A LOVE FOR
GOD

PREFACE

A Love for God is written for everyone. Although those with a basic grasp of both the Old and New Testaments of the Bible will have a better understanding of what I have written, even one without any prior knowledge should be able to, with a Bible at their side, look up the various citations from the Bible, and thereby come to understand the subject quite readily.

There is no history of Bible characters given. There is no explanation given as to creation. It is a book written on the basis that you either already believe in God and the Bible as His written Word, or though you're not quite sure about the Bible being His Word you are willing, with a Bible at your side, to at least look at things from this author's point of view.

A Love for God is a new way of looking at two aspects: Love and God (if one can refer to God as an aspect, just for the purpose of clarification). It does not look from our point of view up to heaven, but from God's point of view down to earth. He is the injured party when it comes to love. The party who has done the injury must therefore listen to the one injured. They do not demand; they listen.

That is what I have tried to do with this book: explain how God longs to be loved, and just how much He loves us. Then I give a practical application in the form of Bible readings, verses to be memorized, as well as verses to meditate on, to help the reader to listen to God, writing His Word in the heart, to cause meditation; to get the reader thinking and moving toward fixing a strained if not broken relationship with God.

All I ask is that you just give it a read with an open mind as if God is communicating to you for the first time as you reference the different Bible passages throughout. Then, apply yourself to the practical application part of the book with the same attitude. My motive is sincere. I do not want you to come to my understanding about a love for God—I want you to come to His.

TABLE OF CONTENTS

CHAPTER I

TRUE LOVE

I do not claim to be an authority on the subject, but I believe God's Word to be.

I will not defend the fact that there is a God by going into long drawn out arguments concerning creation. God doesn't.

He just makes an observation, that only a fool would believe there is no God, and then reveals Himself more fully to those Who seek Him through His written Word.

So that is what I will do in this book. I will seek to understand what it means to have a love for God as revealed through His written Word.

God has revealed that He will hold people who do not believe in Him without excuse if they refuse to acknowledge Him, ignoring the evidence that is in creation, Romans 1:18-20.

One only has to look at creation, study the anatomy of the human body, and consider the psychological makeup that is within a human, to realize we are created beings put upon a world that has been created for us. If you want to argue against that and say everything came about as an accidental explosion, then think on this.

The other day I came upon something that was deposited on a lawn. It had no pattern or design. It was quite apparently an accident. As time had passed and the elements had done their thing, it now was generating outward, making a universe of its own. It was an accident that had been left on the lawn some time ago by some irresponsible dog owner's dog.

I chuckled to myself when I thought, *Even an accident such as this has a creator.*

I digress.

At one time or another, we all were fools.

Perhaps some of us didn't say in our heart that God doesn't exist, but by our lives we certainly made that statement time and again, which I believe to be worse—to claim with the mouth that you aren't a fool, but to display by example that you are indeed a fool.

I write this book then with this single purpose in mind. To have the reader come to an understanding, from God's point of view, what it means to have a love for God.

Do we even know how to love God?

What does it mean to love God?

Does it mean that warm fuzzy feeling you get when you pray at certain times? Does it mean having tears come to your eyes when you sing a particular song? I'm sure those are emotions attached to loving God, but does having those feelings indicate that you love God? Can one have these emotions and not love God?

Yes.

Does it mean assembling every Sunday without fail? Does it mean always taking the Lord's Supper every week? Giving "lotsa" money? Is that a love for God? It can be. But can one do these and not love God?

Yes.

The Pharisees claimed to be good at loving God. They did things like we have just mentioned.

In fact Jesus stated in Matthew 23:23 that the leading religious group of His day, the Pharisees, had all the rules down pat, went through all the motions, even all the emotions that would involve keeping all the rules, but they had forgotten how to have a love for Him. He made it clear that both were necessary; obeying His commands, combining them with love.

I believe God reveals what it means to love Him in many different verses of the Bible, both Old and New Testament. His revelation on love is far different than what our society depicts.

For instance, I know that if a husband wants to love his wife and a wife her husband, each must have the same mind and heart. That's what Ephesians 5 is all about. How does that go? Wives submit to your husbands, as submitting to God; husbands love your wives, just as Christ loved the church. Is that how it reads? Wives submit to your husbands, as submitting to God; husbands—do what?

"How did Christ love the church?"

He gave His life.

"Why? Was it because He loved the church?"

No.

"What? Are you saying Christ didn't love the church?"

No. It states right in the passage we're discussing that Christ loved the church and gave His Life for her. So He loved the church, of that there is no doubt, but the answer given as to how He showed His love was He gave His Life.

So the question we need an answer to is why did He give His life?

He gave His Life because He loved God His Father. He submitted His will to God's will.

The passage is teaching that as husbands, we should be willing to give our lives up for our wives showing we love the Father, submitting our wills to God's will. In reality, both husband and wife submit to each other in submitting to God's will—same mind and heart. In this way, you love God first, each other second, the same as Christ.

"I don't quite get it. Can you teach me more on this love for God?"

Well, I have a better idea of Who can teach us.

Only One. The One mentioned in the passage.

Jesus.

We'll look at His love for God a bit later. But for now, consider this.

Worshipping God has love at its core. You do not worship God out of fear, although fear may be at its beginning. But as you learn more about God, any fear you may have had at the beginning is driven out and replaced with love, based upon the knowledge you attain through His Word about God's love for you. He always loves us first. It is the learned knowledge of His love for us that eventually drives out and replaces our fears.

John wrote in 1 John 4:18, there is no fear in love. Fear has to do with punishment. Perfect or mature love drives out fear. If you still have fear when it comes to loving God, you are still immature and do not understand His love.

It is a different kind of love that is not understood by many, even by those who claim to be God's people. It's a love that is usually misunderstood because many believe that love is connected, and directed, by our feelings. Because many begin with this wrong understanding, their derived conclusions end up wrong.

Let us again refer to the love that is between a man and a woman within marriage. Love that is between that man and woman has nothing to do with feelings. Don't get me wrong. The love that attracts a man to a woman, or a woman to a man has everything to do with feelings, but the love that is commanded by God to keep the marriage going has little if anything to do with feelings.

The love commanded by God is a word that means unconditional service and surrender to another, regardless of how you feel. When two decide to get married, although they may initially want to get married because of emotional love for each other, and may be attracted to each other, and may be burning with passion for each other, both must realize that those feelings will change, but their love does not. They will still unconditionally care and surrender to each other, for the rest of their lives. With that understanding, a bond develops that goes far beyond feeling.

You know that the person you are with will love you in spite of your failings, and you will love them in spite of their failings. Even if they were to become disfigured, or become disabled, you will still love them. This gives glory to God in the highest way, because He still loves us and surrendered His will even to die on a cross to save us, even though we were disabled with sin. We still sin, and grieve Him, but He is still loyal to us, and because He loves us; forgives us.

That is what love between a man and a woman who want to be married should be. You can commit to that without living with each other before marriage. It's not "marriage as long as we like each other, so let's live together to see if we're compatible." It's a marriage based on the same love God has for us. Believe me, sometimes we are very incompatible when it comes to God, yet He doesn't give up on us. Any person you marry will be the right person if you understand what love is. Today's love is a cheap dirty ugly pathetic imitation of the real thing. That's why the divorce rate is so high.

So let's start us all at the beginning.

"What?"

The beginning; let's all start at our own beginning.

"How?"

Well, with this statement.

Everyone at one time or another, did not love God—everyone.

"Huh?"

Please stay with me.

No one is born from mama's womb having a love for God. God loves each of us from the womb, but as a baby you do not have a love for God.

Let me put it another way. Everyone, at one time or another, did not know God. If at one time or another you did not know God, then it is safe to say that at one time or another, each and every one of us did not love God. You cannot love whom you do not know.

Now today we have a problem. There's something that keeps confusing us when we try to find a love for God. Do you know what that is?

It's us.

Yeah, we're the problem.

We each put our own opinion forward as God's opinion. We each think we know what it means to have a love for God, and we each follow our own opinion. Before we will ever understand what it means to have a love for God, we need to get rid of our egos.

How?

Let me explain.

Many may claim to have a love for God, but is that love for God based upon how God longs to be loved?

Is that important to God?

Is it important to you?

Can people love and be wrong?

Of course, they can. It happens all the time. But can people feel in their hearts a genuine, sincere love yet still be wrong? Sadly, the answer can be yes. Here's a little story that explains this.

Many years ago when they sold fabric goods (cloths, linens), they were measured out ahead of time, rolled up, and then sold by the yard.

(Yes, I realize many of my readers won't know what a yard is, so substitute it with a meter. Just remember as we go along that when I refer to a yard it is a unit of measure and not something one plays in.)

Okay then, on with the story.

The linen, or cloths, were measured ahead of time, rolled up, and sold by the yard. Sometimes, a customer would only want half of the roll. Or, they would doubt the proprietor and want the roll measured. So they would take it out, and measure the amount of yardage the customer wanted, or make sure it was exact in length as stated. Instead of using a ruler, or some other type of measuring stick, they would, on the table where they measured the cloth, have two brass tacks nailed into the table that had been measured to be exactly one yard between. The proprietor would then count out a yard each time he stretched the cloth between the two brass tacks, thus measuring out a new length for the customer, or assuring that the length as stated was in fact true. This is where the saying "getting down to the brass tacks" originated.

What? You never heard of that saying? Well, that's where it came from—and you've just heard it.

One young man, who had been handed the family business upon the death of his father, while setting up shop, stretched his measuring tape out between the two tacks and realized they were an inch short (another old unit of measure—look it up).

What was he to do? He knew his father was not a dishonest man. He was certain it was an accident. The tacks had only been placed once as there were no other tell-tale holes. So for forty plus years, his dad had been cheating his customers by one inch every time he measured out a yard. What was he to do? He loved his father, and his father loved the people. If he moved the tack all would see that his father, whether or not on purpose, had been cheating them for all those years. If he left the tack, no one would know. Now tell me. What is the right thing to do? What is the loving thing to do? He knew that if his father had been shown that the measurement was wrong, he would have admitted his error and moved the tack, because he loved his customers. He also knew that if he, as the son, left it as it was, it would not be love for his father or the customers.

The son measured and moved the tack.

What will you do?

Are the "brass tacks" correct?

Do you have a love for God?

If the tacks aren't properly placed, are you willing to move them to show that you have a love for God?

That's why I'm writing this book: to show you how to let God do the measuring. After all, He's the one we want to love, isn't He?

What is the measurement we will be using?

No, it is not metric.

Here's the measurement we'll be using.

It's universal.

It works with metric as well.

In John 17:17 Jesus, as He prays to God, asks His Father to sanctify His followers by the Truth, and then states that God's Word is the Truth.

Okay. First off, what does sanctify mean? Let's just go by the modern dictionary definition.

It means to make something holy; free somebody from sin; bless something through religious vow; officially approve something; make something route to holiness.

Let's see now.

That would then become, make them holy by the Truth. Your Word is Truth.

What does holy mean?

It means to set apart as special or different; dedicated for one special purpose.

Let's try that again.

Make them special, make them set apart; make them different for a special purpose, by the Truth. Your Word is Truth.

Jesus wants God to make us different, set apart from others, by using God's Word as the measuring rod—or "brass tacks".

That means if I read God's Word and do what it says, I will be different, automatically, because I'm following His will, which will set me apart from those who don't follow His will. It has nothing to do with being better than other people, but it has everything to do with being different, or set apart.

Now wait a minute.

Does it have to be exactly as God's Word states? Has God always expected this of those who claim to have a love for Him?

Let's let God answer that by referencing some Scripture.

CHAPTER 2

KNOWLEDGE, ZEAL, AND BEING EXACT

In Hosea 4:6, the prophet Hosea states a message from God to the effect that His people, Israel, were about to be destroyed because they had a lack of knowledge. In other words, they had a lack of the Truth; God's Word.

Furthermore, in Malachi 2:7, the prophet Malachi goes on to state that the priests whom God had appointed, were responsible for the preservation of the knowledge from God, and all were to look to them for instruction, as they were the messengers of God. So in other words, they spoke God's Truth.

You see, the tribe of Levi served as priests for God. They, together with the High Priest, took care of the temple and all of the sacrifices. They also were in charge of addressing God's statutes to the people. Israel had abandoned God's Law. The priests had stopped teaching it. As a result Israel had become worse than the nations around her. God decided to discipline Israel by allowing her to fall captive to other nations. Yet when God addresses Israel through His prophet Hosea, He reveals that all of the people are destroyed through lack of knowledge.

"Say what? Why all the people? It's not everyone's fault the priests weren't doing their job."

Wait a minute now. Where does God say it's the people's fault, other than the priests, that everyone's being destroyed? He's not saying the people will be destroyed because they didn't take the time to read the Old Testament Law. He's revealing the natural consequence of the priests not doing what they were responsible for!

It's like this.

Say there's a mine field. Say only three people out of thirty who have to cross it know where the live mines are. Say the three have been given the responsibility to instruct the other twenty-seven as to how to cross the mine field safely. But they don't. The thirty cross, and as a result everyone is destroyed by the blasts of the mines going off, even the ones who knew, because they're with the people and die in the explosions.

On the other side, their commander makes this observation, "They were all destroyed because they had a lack of knowledge."

He's not laying any blame on the ones who had no idea where the mines were. He's just making a statement that they were all destroyed because the initial three didn't carry out the responsibilities given them. Had they done so, the entire thirty would have crossed safely.

Okay?

Same with God and His people; because the priests rejected knowledge; because they ignored His Law, their children will be ignored.

"What? Why? What do the children have to do with this? Why blame them?"

He isn't.

It's the same thing.

He's ignoring the priests because they rejected Him by rejecting His Law. They didn't know God and what He wanted because they stopped inquiring of Him. They stopped following the Law. As a consequence, the children haven't been taught, so—get it?

As a natural consequence, because the children haven't been taught, they'll be ignored also because they can't follow something they haven't been taught! Let's lay the blame where it's deserved. It's the leaders who were to teach the Law to their children. They neglected doing so, so now their children do as they please also, not following the Law of God, so they too will end up being ignored.

"That's kind of mean. Why doesn't God just teach them Himself?"

There's a deep answer for that question, but let's just give the simple answer. He already tried that! How do you think the priests learned? He taught them through the Law. Where does it end? Can't God's people be responsible?

What would you do as a school principal if your grade nine teacher came to you and said she/he is going to have to teach her/his entire class grade eight because the grade eight teacher didn't do his/her job? Would you say, "Now, now—I'll do it"? Then as you're doing that, the grade ten teacher says, "I'll have to teach the grade nines all over from the beginning of grade nine because the grade nine teacher didn't have time to teach them grade nine." Would you get the idea that some of the teachers didn't give a hoot about the students, or you as the principal? They know the rules, they just don't care!

They don't care about you, they don't care about the students—what would you do? Hmmm. I can see some teachers looking for new jobs as a natural consequence. I can see students being handicapped when it comes to knowledge. I can see a mess.

God's people were a mess. They had no knowledge of God.

Now, let's go back to the Scripture from the Old Testament (Malachi 2:7) which we previously referred to. Remember, the priests of that time were responsible to all who would seek guidance from God. They were to instruct all people according to the Word of God; according to the Truth, as God delivered it to His priests.

Now, let's bring this up to date, to New Covenant/Testament times.

In 1Peter 2:9, Peter writes that all Christians are now priests, and all Christians are responsible to declare God's Word, the Truth. In fact it states that Christians have been chosen, by God, for just that purpose.

Uh oh.

Then according to this verse all Christians will be held responsible for teaching God's Word correctly.

In view of this, I have some questions:

What will happen if we follow the example given of God's priests in Hosea 4:6?

What if anyone, for instance the religious leaders in the community, ignore what is contained in God's Word, and teach something else, or nothing at all?

What about the people who will follow them?

Won't they have a lack of knowledge? And if they have a lack of knowledge, won't they then be destroyed?

"But how can that be? Many are zealous for God. Just because they don't know what God wants they'll be destroyed? No, that's Old Testament stuff."

Excuse me?

We just referred to a verse from the New Testament, 1Peter 2:9.

There's more.

In Romans 10:1-2, the apostle Paul, as Inspired by the Holy Spirit, writes that his desire and prayers were for the salvation of the Israelites. But to his sorrow he states that although Israel is zealous for God, their zeal is not based on knowledge. Sound familiar? Zeal means enthusiasm; fervor; excitement. Paul is stating that though the Israelites are serving God with great enthusiasm; fervor, it is not based on knowledge from God, and so although they are zealous for God, they are lost.

Further on, in verse 21 of Romans 10, Paul states that God views the zeal of Israel as them being disobedient and stubborn toward Him.

So that means they could be praying fervently, singing joyously, with great zeal for God, yet He views them as disobedient, because it is not according to His Truth.

Are you still with me? Is that kind of hard to take? Well, let me explain further.

This was a statement as to how it was in the first century. The Israelites were zealous for God, but they rejected the Old Testament prophets who spoke about the Christ. They didn't want to listen to God, Who was now revealing to them the New Testament through the apostles' teachings who had been taught by Christ and empowered by His Spirit, that Jesus was the Messiah, their Savior. But they didn't like what they heard, so they stayed with the Old Law. They were zealous for God—but lost.

That's not how God wanted it. God wants all to come to the knowledge of the Truth and be saved. You can read that in 1Timothy 2:4.

"Well, what is it with God? If I love Him in my heart and my feelings are sincere, yet just because I don't read the Bible and do what He says, you're saying I don't love Him?"

No. Not necessarily. You may love Him indeed, in your own way. Here's an example.

Let's say you meet this girl you really like. I'm going to do this coming from the man's point of view because, well, I'm a man. To show her you love her you take her to all the football games you go to. You buy her hotdogs, snacks; you make sure she can watch the game from a good seat. When it rains you make sure you have hot chocolate and nice warm coats. You love her, and this shows you love her. But she doesn't seem to be happy. So you buy her flowers, buy a nice big house. Stock it with all the modern conveniences. Take her on trips all around the world. You love her, and this shows you love her. But she doesn't seem to be happy. All the while she's been going to the games because she loves you; she doesn't like them at all. She accepted all the gifts lavished on her, because she observed that it made you happy. But she didn't want any of them. All this time you've been thinking you were expressing your love for her, but it turns out, she has been expressing her love for you. All she wanted was to just once do something that was important to her; for you to take the time to observe what she liked to do. Maybe take a walk together. Go window shopping together. Watch a romantic movie with a bowl of popcorn. Go out to a coffee shop to have a cup and just talk.

Yeah, yeah, yeah. Blah, blah, blah.

You've heard all that before.

Then why don't you listen?

You're expressing love for her the way you think she wants to be loved instead of listening and learning how she longs to be loved. Are you making the same mistake with God? Are you expressing love for Him the way you think He wants to be loved? Why don't you take the time to learn? In both cases, failing to learn may truly cost you the relationship.

"Ahhhh. God's bigger than that. He knows my heart."

You're right. He does. And that's the problem.

Let's try to get an understanding of what is important to God. Maybe if we observe Him, we can learn from Him. It'll be quick and maybe leave some holes. But I think you'll get a good idea just from a brief overview.

In Exodus 25:9 God commands Moses to make the tabernacle and all its furnishings, exactly according to the pattern He was going to give them. The tabernacle was the house of God; where He would be worshipped. The furnishings were all the vessels and tools that would be used in that worship.

In Numbers 8:4 we have an example of one of the lamp stands being made of hammered gold exactly as the pattern had been given to Moses by God.

In Numbers 15:14 God states that in generations to come, when it came to sacrifices being made to God by fire, whether Israelite or alien, everyone must do it exactly as God instructed.

So, God laid out the commands to Moses as to the tabernacle where He will be worshipped, as well as all the utensils that will be used in worship under the Old Covenant. Going back to the original language, a word is used here that means "to not deviate". Some translate this to mean "precise" or perhaps "exact".

This is important to God. He wants no deviation.

If Moses were to deviate, what would that betray about his heart?

If he does it precisely, what would that reveal?

Have you ever heard these words from your wife/husband when you bought him/her something they asked for?

"Oh, it's exactly what I wanted! It matches perfectly! Right down to the trim along the bottom! Precisely what I asked for! Ohhh, I love you!"

No?

Maybe I shouldn't be surprised.

Let's move on.

In the New Covenant God expects those under it to be the same in following His Word exactly. In Hebrews 8:1-6 it is written that as the Old

Covenant and its system of worship was but a shadow of what was going to be under the New Covenant, that we should be all the more careful to do exactly as God commands, because the New Covenant/Testament is superior to the Old Covenant/Testament in that it is founded on better promises.

Go ahead, grab your copy of the Bible, and look up Hebrews 8:1-6. The original language in which the New Testament was written relates the idea that the New Testament is "the real", while the Old Testament was "the pattern". The Old was sort of a shadowy image of the New. The idea being that the "real" is always more important than the "pattern". The original language also quite clearly states that the New Covenant is founded on much better promises, making it superior. Again, perhaps your Bible uses some of these words.

Seeing as the New Covenant/Testament is superior/better, do you think it might be important that we follow it exactly also? Okay, again—an example.

Someone is racing down the road on a bike. If you stand in the way you'll get hit, so you'd best get out of the way.

Someone is racing down the road in a car. If you stand in the way you'll get hit, so you'd best get out of the way.

Someone is racing down the road in a truck. If you stand in the way you'll get hit, so you'd best get out of the way.

Someone is racing down the road in one of those dragsters. If you stand in the way you'll get hit, so you'd best get out of the way.

Someone is racing down the road in one of those rocket fueled rockets—

Egads!

Do you get the idea? In the case of the bike, if you stand in the way, you'll get hurt. As we move down the line, as the vehicle gets superior, it becomes even more important to get out of the way! You'll really get hurt, maybe even die! Duh! Ya think?

What was true of the Old Testament is even more so of the superior New Testament.

With everything, what is true of the lesser is even more so true of the greater.

If you don't believe me, let's go out to that road.

I'll be brave and stand in front of the bike.

You'll be brave and stand in front of the rocket powered rocket.

I may have to go to the hospital.

They'll be picking you up, piece by piece, in a body bag. Let's keep moving—quickly!

While you have your Bible handy, check out Philippians 3:17. There the apostle Paul commands the believers to follow his example, and to take special notice of those who live in accordance with the pattern he had given them.

In 2Timothy 1:13, he commands Timothy who he is training to be an evangelist, that he is to keep what he has heard from Paul as the tupos of sound teaching. "Tupos" is a Greek word that means "a pattern to be followed".

So let's see now...

Make everything according to the pattern to be followed.

The New Covenant is superior to the old one.

It is founded on better promises.

Live according to the pattern we gave you.

What you heard from me, keep as the pattern of sound teaching.

See the similarities?

Now, when God states something, is He serious?

When I say God, keep in mind that He is speaking through His apostle. When Paul writes, it is Inspired by God; it's literally God's Word.

God is not like men. He doesn't change His mind. He doesn't lie. He doesn't state He's going to do something then without reason not do it. When He promises, that promise is always kept. That's how I understand the words used in Numbers 23:19.

Again, in 1Samuel 15:29, He does not lie, nor change His mind without reason, like a man might.

He's not a man. Not anything like a man. So don't put the way you think about things on Him.

You need to find out the way He thinks about things, and put them on you!

"Yeah, but Jesus is not as hardnosed as God was."

Excuse me?

Jesus is God. Read John 1:1. He became flesh in order to live here on earth with us, John 1:14. His Words spoken while He was here were the very Words of God...the Truth. The Words He spoke while on earth will be the very Words that will either save us or condemn us, according to John 12:47-50.

Don't take my word for it, read it! There's no reason why you should end up outside of God's favor because of a lack of knowledge.

Hello?

Are you still reading...?

What I'm getting at is Jesus and God is One and the Same.

So it has nothing to do with being hardnosed. And what is this "hard-nosed"? Is that what you call your husband/wife when they get angry at you because you don't love them the way they want to be loved?

"Ahhhh, she's just hardnosed, I'm going to the football game."

Whew!

I better calm down.

Wait! Wait! What's that? I hear another question.

"How can God say He doesn't change His mind when we've gone from being in a relationship with Him in the garden of Eden to being banished from the garden, to being under an Old Covenant, then 'changing' to a New Covenant? He's always 'changing' His mind!"

We went from a relationship with Him in the garden huh. What a pleasant way of putting it.

Didn't Adam and Eve have something to do with that? Weren't they the ones who "changed" things?

I've never been under the Old Covenant—I'm not Jewish. I was a Gentile. I was an alien and a stranger in the world with no hope at all of life after death. At least that's how I understand what is written in Ephesians 2:11-22.

But regardless, in Ephesians 1:3-10 God makes it very clear that He intended to save all who are in Jesus Christ even before the creation of the world.

Go ahead and read that passage before you move on in this book. It's quite a long passage, but it reveals that God has never changed His mind about this. From the beginning, even before the beginning, He was planning to save us in Christ so we could be with Him eternally. That, my friends, is love.

"Yeah, okay. But you say in order to love God we have to learn what loving God is all about. What if I don't like the way God loves me? What if my way of God loving me is to let me do what I want?"

He is letting you do what you want. You've just answered the age-old question, "If there is a loving God, why doesn't He interfere?"

He's not interfering because He loves you. If the way you want to be loved is to do things the way you want to do them with no holds barred, He allows you to. You see? He loves you the way you want to be loved.

Now, if you want to love God, won't you do the same? Love Him the way He wants to be loved?

The consequences are: You keep doing things the way you want; God will love you and not interfere; however, it will cost you your soul, if that's what you want.

Do things God's way and learn to love Him, and it will save your soul, if that's what you want.

To me, it's a no-brainer.

"But why does that make me such a bad person? I'm not a murderer. I'm not a thief. I'm not a cold-blooded-psycho-war-monger."

Ahhhh, now I see where you're going with this. That's okay, because many struggle with this same idea. Most people are good within the community they live. They keep their lawns cut, their yards clean; they give to local charities and pay their taxes. They are law-abiding citizens. Before I go further, let's again turn to God's Word; the Truth. His Word was recorded in the past for the specific reason of answering questions that would come in the future.

CHAPTER 3
GOD'S PERSPECTIVE

Many things were written down to serve as examples for us, to teach us, to encourage hope within us. You don't believe me? Read for yourself. Go ahead. Don't just sit there staring at these words in this book. Verify what I'm saying by turning to 1Corinthians 10:1-11, and then Romans 15:4, and read.

Go ahead...

I'm waiting...

See?

Now, let's look at what was written in the past that we might learn.

Do people suffer before God simply because of a lack of knowledge?

Does God mean "exactly" when He says "exactly"?

Does God change His commands to suit people, or does He expect people to change to suit His commands?

Let's take a little trip. We'll start from King David, because most everyone is familiar with the man who killed Goliath and was claimed by God to be the apple of His eye. But I want to refer to a part of David's life where he wasn't such an "apple". You see, David usually went off to war with his men. But one time he decided to stay back. He was up on the roof and he noticed a woman by the name of Bathsheba bathing. He watched her, desired her, and though he knew she was married, had her brought to him and he lay with her. She became pregnant. David, to cover his sin of adultery, had Uriah, Bathsheba's husband, brought in from battle. He was hoping Uriah would lay with his wife, and then the pregnancy would be thought of as his. But he refused to even go to his wife. He thought it would be a disgrace to have such luxury while the other men were out on the battlefield. So David got him drunk, but he still refused to be with his wife. So David sent Uriah back to battle and commanded his officer Joab to put him in the front line so he would be killed. Well, it worked. Bathsheba, now by law released from her marriage to Uriah because of death, married David.

For some time his sin went unnoticed, that is, by man. Nathan, God's prophet, approached David one day and confronted him of these very sins. You can read about it in 2Samuel 12:7-18. There God states that David's actions were as if he despised God's Word, as if he despised God Himself. Because David did this evil God pronounces three judgments. One, the sword would never depart from his house. Number two, his own wives would be taken, and given to someone close to him. Though he did this in secret with Bathsheba, his wives would lie with someone in broad daylight. Three, the child conceived in adultery would die.

Keep in mind this is the David whom God saw as the apple of His Eye. It's important to understand this, for it impresses upon us that God's love does not show favoritism.

Now, consider how God loved David. He anointed him as king over Israel. He gave everything over to him.

Now consider how David loved God in return for this. He committed adultery with Bathsheba, had Uriah killed then took her to be his own.

God considers David's actions as him despising God's Word, and despising God Himself.

As a result, because God in His love does not show favoritism; because God cares for Uriah the Hittite's family and relatives as well; because David has not only been unloving toward God (despised Him and His Word is how the Hebrew text reads) but has been unjust toward Uriah, God will be the rod of justice.

Did God do "exactly" as He said He would?

Yes.

The child died on the seventh day.

Absalom, David's own son lay with his wives in a tent pitched on a roof so all Israel could see.

Absalom died by the sword.

Go ahead and read about it in 2Samuel 12:18; 16:20-22; 18:14-15.

While we're with David, let's look a little earlier in his life.

Turn back, while you have your Bible open, to 2Samuel 6:3-9.

Go ahead...

Here you will read about David bringing the ark of God from the house of Abinadab. This was the Ark of the Covenant that had the golden cherubim, angels, on the top with outstretched wings pointing toward each other. God dwelt over the Ark when it was in the Holy of Holies, that area of the temple where God manifested himself and that only the High Priest could enter. Try and picture this. They're carrying the Ark on a new cart, not an old cart, but a new one. It had to be a new cart because after all, the Ark was Holy, sacred. Uzzah and Ahio, sons of Abinadab, were guiding the cart, with Ahio in the front, and Uzzah alongside. Everyone thought this was a great idea! David and the whole house of Israel were celebrating with all their might, with all kinds of instruments, praising God very zealously for this great event. When they came to a certain threshing floor, the oxen that were pulling the cart stumbled. It seems the Ark may fall off, so Uzzah reached out his hand to steady it. The Lord becomes angry at this because to Him it was an irreverent act, so God struck him down and he died on that spot.

Why an irreverent act? What was wrong with this? Seems natural; the Ark of God on a new cart. Not just some old thing. A new cart, because after all, it was the Ark of God. The whole house of Israel, along with David, seems to think everything's okay. The oxen stumble, Uzzah, perhaps a reflex action, steadies the Ark, and— what?! Why?

Why call it an irreverent act? Did Uzzah know this? I'm not sure. Maybe someone forgot to remind Uzzah. Maybe due to lack of knowledge—did anyone know?

Well, it seems that according to 1Chronicles 15:2, David may have known why. Did he forget? Did he find this out later? Or, did he know but just took for granted that God wouldn't mind? When you love someone, do you just take for granted that what you think is all right will be all right with them?

Hmmmm.

Let's go back further, to Moses. Turn back to Numbers 20 and read verses 2-12. Go ahead, read Numbers 20:2-12.

Ready?

Ok, so they're out of water. The people are grumbling. God instructs Moses to take his staff, gather the assembly together, speak to a rock, and that rock would bring forth water. Enough water for the whole community as well as the livestock to be satisfied. So Moses does as God told him. He gathers the people together in front of the rock, calls the people rebels, raises his arm and strikes the rock twice. The water gushed forth, enough, just as God said, to satisfy the whole community as well as the livestock. Then take special note of what God stated to Moses and Aaron. He reveals to them His perspective of their actions. He stated that by doing what they did they did not trust Him, they did not consider Him holy, and because of this they would not bring the people into the Promised Land.

Let's look closely at this.

What was God's will?

Speak to the rock.

What did Moses do?

He struck the rock twice with his staff.

Okay, so if anything I'd call that "getting ahead of myself" or at the worst "disobedience." Just because I didn't do "exactly" as He said...

How did God view it?

The Hebrew has the idea of having a lack of faith in God, of treating Him as common, rather than special. Your version of the Bible may use similar words, but we get the idea that this, to God, was very disrespectful, to say the least.

Therefore:

Moses and Aaron, you will not bring this community into the Promised Land.

Wait now.

Moses is the man!

He spoke face to face with God, brought down the Ten Commandments— God really loves this guy.

Yet, no favoritism.

Did God mean what He said?

This is very important now that you read these verses. I want you to let God communicate these events to you through His Word. We're trying to find out what it means to have a love for God. So if you've just been reading along without a Bible, go and get a copy of the Scriptures, a Bible, and read all these passages.

Now turn to Deuteronomy 32:48-52. God allows Moses to view the Promised Land, but true to His Word, Moses will not take the people into the land. Aaron has already died, so he too did not cross over into the land.

God does not speak and then change His mind when it comes to judgment and justice.

I don't know what you call what Moses and Aaron did, but I'd call it a slip, a little disobedience.

But from God's perspective, and we get something new from this last passage, it was because they both broke faith with Him, neither of them thought it important enough to treat what God told them to do as holy.

Remember, we're trying to learn things from God's perspective. We want to know how to love God. He already knows how to love us. That has never been, and never will be, the problem.

God is not a man. He doesn't lie. He doesn't change His mind. When He speaks He acts. When He promises He fulfills. As so stated in Numbers 23:19 and 1Samuel 15:29.

These examples should help you understand other passages recorded in the Old Testament.

At first glance God's judgment may seem harsh, but if you get to know God, you will see that His judgments are always fair and for the good of mankind as a whole.

Even with Noah and the flood, or even all the way back to Adam and Eve, the judgments made were for the good of mankind as a whole, and were because people, or even two people, weren't obeying His commands. They, by their actions, did not love God.

Now let's go back to a certain question...

"But why does that make me such a bad person? I'm not a murderer. I'm not a thief. I'm not a cold-blooded-psycho-war-monger."

Do the passages we just looked at together help you understand now?

Do you understand that by actions a person can reveal that they do not have a love for God, yet still be a good person like Moses?

That if you fail to carry out what God wants, from His perspective you don't care about Him?

What do you mean that's not fair?

So I can tell you I care about you then totally ignore what you want? Is that what you're saying?

Let's review: what is true of the lesser, is even more so of the greater. Remember? That's where we broke off.

We've looked at several examples that show God's people, no matter who they were, could not ignore the Old Covenant, the lesser.

So the New Covenant, the greater, is it something we can ignore?

God's people could not change the Old Covenant, the lesser.

So the New Covenant, the greater, is it something we can change?

Under the Old Covenant, the lesser, if God's people rejected it, God rejected them.

So under the New Covenant, the greater, if we reject it, will God reject us?

Regardless as to whether we are murderers, or thieves, or cold-blooded-psycho-war-mongers, or law abiding citizens, if we reject what is written in God's New Testament, He will reject us.

Does that make you uncomfortable? Well when you love someone, aren't you willing to feel uncomfortable at times in order to win their heart? Should our love for God always be what we're comfortable with? What about from His perspective?

Jesus, as He speaks to the Pharisees in the New Testament, the leading religious faction of His day, revealed they did not have a love for God because they weren't following God's will, even though they claimed they were.

The apostles who were taught by Jesus and guided directly by the Holy Spirit also have the same message…to have a love for God means loving God the way He wants to be loved.

Let's pause here for a moment. Let's consider some things, just for a moment.

My intention is that this book will bring you peace, not make you uncomfortable. Yet sometimes when we learn things that we "kinda" already know but hate to see in black and white, it makes us uncomfortable—especially if we're seen to be in the group who thought they were loving God, but turn out not to be loving Him at all.

My desire is that you will truly find out what it means to love God. Only that will usher in a peace to your life that you have never thought possible.

That is what you want, isn't it?

You do want to love God the way He wants to be loved, don't you?

Or is this a one-way street? God must love you the way you want, and you will love God the way you want.

Do you really want to love God the way He wants you to love Him?

That's what you have to decide.

So then, the human race is not only seen as not loving God because they're murderers, or thieves, or cold-blooded-psycho-war-mongers.

It's also because they don't follow God's will. Needless to say, those just mentioned most definitely do not follow God's will. We call it "not following God's will." But what does God call it? How does it look from His perspective?

Enough considering, enough of a pause…here we go again.

In Deuteronomy 13:1-5, God reveals that at times He does things to see if we really love Him. Now God already knows our hearts, but in these verses, He, is revealing to us, what it means to love Him. Go ahead. Don't just take my word for it. Turn to the passage I just mentioned and read it. God will allow a false prophet to come along and introduce false teachings to see if someone who claims to love Him with all their heart and with all their soul really does. He also states within this passage, that anyone who teaches anything that is not a part of God's Will, that person is rebellious.

God refers to a false prophet teaching things that God has not commanded as being a rebel.

What is rebellion to God? How bad can that be?

Well, I found another passage that dealt with rebellion, but it revealed something quite astounding. It was 1Samuel 15:23. In this passage, according to the Hebrew, or the Septuagint (the Greek translation of the Old Testament) God likens rebellion to seeking advice from other gods. What words does your version use? The Hebrew states that God considers rebellion as one chasing after other divine beings, to set up an idol. In other words, if you're not listening to Him you're listening to some other Divine being. There are no other gods besides Him, so you must be worshipping a false-god, an idol, and putting that idol above God!

Let's state that again.

God looks at preaching differently or going against His Words as rebellion; He looks at rebellion as seeking knowledge by some other divine means other than by His Word.

Divination means to seek knowledge by supernatural means, the method or practice of attempting to foretell the future or discovering the unknown through omens, oracles, or supernatural powers.

Idolatry, of course, is worshipping an idol.

Wow! Did you know God felt that way about rebellion?

There's another example in Jeremiah 28:15-16. A false prophet by the name of Hananiah persuades the whole nation to trust in lies. God, through His prophet Jeremiah predicts that because he has done so, because he preached rebellion, that very year he would die.

Whoa! He persuaded the nation to trust in lies, and from God's perspective it is direct rebellion against Him.

Well then, how does God define rebellion...exactly?

Look no further than Isaiah 30:9. There it is stated that rebellious people are those people who are deceitful, those unwilling to listen to the Lord's instruction.

So from God's perspective, being unwilling to listen to His Word is rebellion and deceit.

Now those are Old Testament examples. Does He still look at it the same way? Has His perspective changed in the New Testament?

Not according to Titus 1:9-11. There the apostle Paul, Inspired by the Holy Spirit, writes to his evangelist in training that there were some rebellious people who were ruining whole Christian households by teaching things that were not God's Words.

So it seems that it's the same for us under the New Covenant.

"Yeah but still, we're looking at people who were preaching something different than God, who are in active rebellion against God. I'm not like that."

But we just read that not doing God's will is also viewed as rebellion.

You didn't read it did you? Go ahead. Read Isaiah 30:9. These people don't view themselves as rebellious. They just don't listen to God's instruction as it was given to them. They're not "bad" people perhaps as we might view "bad". But we're not supposed to be looking at this topic from only our point of view, remember? The reason you bought this book was to find out how God wants to be loved, remember? Or...

"Okay. Fine. I understand that. Still, I don't believe I'm like they were. I mean. I may not do everything He teaches, but I try to be good. Do you have an example that is more like what I'm trying to say?"

Maybe; well, no, I don't. But, perhaps—

Jesus does.

Turn to your New Testament. Now please do. Don't take for granted what I write. Read it in your Bible for yourself. In Luke 16:19-29 we have a parable, told by Jesus, of a certain rich man and a beggar named Lazarus. Go ahead and read it. It's a bit long, but go ahead, I have time. I'll wait while you do.

Go on...

Read it...

This is a parable. Parables are designed to teach spiritual truths.

This rich man is not described as preaching something different. He doesn't seem to be in active rebellion. Or was he? Remember, from God's perspective, rebellion is being unwilling to listen to Him.

Did you know that there is a command given by God under the Old Covenant that states all those who were part of God's nation were to be generous to the poor? Whether they were of Israel or strangers? It's true. Read Deuteronomy 15:11.

Now notice from the passage. Is this rich man described as a bad man? I guess it depends on your perception. He wasn't a murderer, or a war-monger, but he did ignore Lazarus who was right at his gate. He had to pass Lazarus every time he went out. Lazarus even longed for crumbs. Now the explanation for this ignorance could be one of two reasons.

The priests had failed to communicate God's Word to His people, which would include this rich man so he did not have knowledge, putting him into the group of not having knowledge.

Or the priests had properly communicated God's Word and he just didn't listen to the command which would then put him into the rebellious group.

This rich man would not be seen by close friends as being without knowledge or rebellious. In fact, take note of the man's attitude while in torment. It is to say the least...admirable. There is no anger. He just wants to warn his brothers. By him wanting to warn his brothers he acknowledges that his brothers are doing something wrong, just as he was.

He doesn't even ask to leave the torment and warn them himself, he asks Abraham to send Lazarus.

But Abraham's response is that his brothers have the same to heed as he had; Moses and the Prophets. They would get no special treatment. God's Word, as given by Moses and the Prophets, was enough.

Whom do we have? Hebrews 1:1-2 makes it clear we have the Words of Jesus Christ.

Well what about Jesus? How did He love God?

Jesus equated a love for God as doing exactly what His Father, God, commanded; which is not just my opinion. It's the Words of Jesus Himself and can be found in John 14:31. A Greek word is used here that by definition means "precise" or "exact". Which word does your Bible use? You need to read that. Go ahead. Turn to John 14 and read verse 31.

Amazing, isn't it?

Jesus knew that to love God was the same as what God stated all down through the course of time.

To love the Father is to do exactly what He has commanded.

Loving God is to obey His commands.

Jesus' primary incentive for going to the cross was not love for the world but love for the Father.

Now understand what I've just written.

His primary incentive for going to the cross was not love for the world; it was love for the Father.

Although Jesus loved the lost, and He came to seek and to save the lost, it was not stated that Jesus so loved the world that He gave His life.

It was stated that God so loved the world that He gave His one and only Son.

Jesus so loved His Father that He gave His Life for the sins of mankind, regardless of how He felt, and in the Garden of Gethsemane He didn't feel too good about it. Remember while He prayed? While His disciples slept, isn't it revealed that he asked the Father to take the cup He was about to drink away from Him? Yet didn't He conclude that prayer with Him relinquishing His Will to His Father's Will?

The primary incentive was Jesus' love for God, not His love for the world.

In like manner, if we love the Father, we will surrender our will to His will no matter how we may feel.

Need more?

Read John chapters 14 and 15. There you will find a love for God being attached to phrases such as "obey My commands", "obey My teaching".

You need to read those chapters.

Please...

Stop reading this book and read those chapters.

Thank you.

Now one more Scripture, that puts it all into black and white. Let's let John, one of the apostles, as guided by the Holy Spirit, sum it all up. Turn in your copy of the Scriptures to 1 John 5:3 and read.

You cannot get any clearer than that.

Soooooo ...

If it is your heart's desire to love the Lord with all your heart, mind, and soul, then it's necessary to obey His commands.

"But that's so ... so ... how would I put it? So unfeeling; like a robot."

Really?

So when you show that you love your wife and do what she wants to do, and it makes her happy and you can tell it makes her happy, there's no joy inside of you? You're just like a robot, going through the motions?

Tell me, honestly. Do you want to love, or just be loved?

If you are selfish and only want to be loved, then yes, when you are trying to love someone else and doing what they like, you will be like a robot.

But if you truly desire to make the other person happy, to really love the other person, then you will find joy in doing what they want because you know that's what makes them happy. You know it's for their good, not yours.

Now of course we must be careful, for there are people who will abuse that and say things like...

"If you love me, you'll do whatever I like."

Then they may command you to do things that are immoral. But you see? If you put love for God first, you can say to that person…

"But we're both to love God first, and put our love for each other second, and what you're asking me to do puts you in first place because it's against God's commands, so no, I won't do that."

Isn't that great?

That's what's so unique about God wanting to be loved the way He reveals. Because—now get this—even when He asks us to love Him by obeying His commands, even that is to protect us. He created us. He knows what is best for us. He knows what will hurt us.

There are thieves out there. They'll tell you they love you, but they really want to steal your heart mind and soul for themselves. They don't want to love back; they just want to be loved.

That's why I asked, "Do you want to love, or just be loved?"

It identifies who you are. If you only want to be loved, and don't want to take the time to love, then you are taking something without giving anything back, and that makes you a thief.

When such thieves promise, "I'll always love you," it's not sincere.

When you give them your love, you will eventually find that what they promised was a lie.

You'll end up feeling not only unloved, but unfulfilled.

So when He asks you to love Him by obeying His commands, He's really saying love Him first so that you will find true love in your own life. If you put Him first, you will obey His commands, which will protect you from the thieves, and you will have life and have it to the full.

That's the kind of love Jesus has for you. He makes it clear that when those who do not want to love but only want to be loved claim they love you, their real intent is to kill and destroy. He came so that you could have a real, full life. You can read that in John 10:10.

See?

So when you obey God you are demonstrating a love for God. That relationship with God will protect you from those who say they love you, but don't.

So even obedience to God is in fact Him still loving you!

You're obeying because you want to show Him you love Him, but He's asking you to obey because He knows the thieves are out there after your soul. He wants you to obey so you'll be protected from them because He loves you.

He also knows that if you are outside of His love, the best you can look forward to is an eternity without Him. To have an eternity without God means an eternity without any good, just evil. For only God is good. God is light; in Him there is no darkness at all. Remove God, and all you have left is darkness and evil—for an eternity.

But He will allow you that choice, because to force you to love Him is not love.

Love can only be exercised by a willing heart.

There are many people out there who have fallen in love with the thief. Christ referred to them as "lost sheep."

You might be one of them.

If you are, even now, God loves you.

He came to rescue you.

But you have to want to be rescued. In order to be rescued you must see yourself as one needing to be rescued, for according to Luke 19:10, that is precisely why He came to earth.

"That seems harsh. If what you're saying is true, then there are a lot of people who don't love God, and are lost, because no one reads their Bible anymore. Or if they read it, they don't follow it. You trying to tell me people are lost simply because they don't obey a command?"

No.

It's because they don't love God.

Have you forgotten so quickly?

Remember how God described people who were rebellious and deceitful? Didn't He state that anyone who was unwilling to listen to His Word were just that, rebellious and deceitful?

Did you actually turn to those Scriptures and read them?

You need to. If you just read this book and not turn to the Scriptures you'll never accept it as the Lord's Will.

You need to read them.

Jesus statement in John 14:31 makes it very clear that for Him to have a love for God meant doing exactly as His Father commanded.

Please get a Bible, turn to that Scripture, and read it.

The apostle John, in the Bible, in his letter that is entitled 1 John, in chapter 5 and verse 3 actually states that to have a love for God is to obey His commands. It can't be stated any clearer.

Please turn to that Scripture in your Bible, and read it.

We can make failing to obey God's command sound so innocent: "simply because they don't obey a command."

It never has been "simply because they don't obey a command."

It has always been, we fail to love Him because we fail in the knowledge of what it means to love Him.

"Okay, okay. But what I mean is I think you're making it more serious than it really is."

Really?

Me?

Or God?

Ever hear of a couple named Adam and Eve? How many commands did they break to get booted out of paradise?

"Yeah, yeah, but that's only two. I don't believe that millions are going to be lost."

Actually it affected all of mankind. But that's another topic.

Ever hear of someone named Noah?

I'm going to ask you to read another passage, 2Peter 3:3-7. This refers us back to the time of Noah and the flood. I've done some personal research on this. Let me share it with you.

From my personal study of the Old Testament Scriptures regarding this event it seems the average size of the family was four to seven children. The way I derived these figures when it comes to children per family was found in the book of Genesis where it indicates more than once that each family had at least four children. How does it indicate that? When it states that each person had "sons and daughters." Since it is "sons and daughters" (plural), one can assume a minimum of two sons and two daughters. But Genesis also records Adam and Eve having seven children. So then, using this information, a reasonable value would appear to be a range of four to seven children per family. Therefore, using four to seven children per family, one can estimate the world population at Noah's time to be, at the very least, 2 billion, and at the very most 11.5 billion. Now I realize this is not factoring in premature or natural death. But even if we were to give up half to death (which would seem to be extreme), this would still leave a population of at the very least 1 billion, and at the very most 5.75 billion.

Even at the very least, 1 billion, 1Peter 3:20 states only eight people were saved. The population was so wicked, only 8 were saved…out of 1 billion, with the possibility of 8 out of 6 billion…that's 8 out of 6,000,000,000.

Now, He did it once, with water. Next time according to 2Peter 3:7 it will be fire.

How? How could several billion people become ungodly? How could several billion people not have a love for God?

CHAPTER 4

A LIAR FROM THE BEGINNING

Adam and Eve loved God. Someone stole their love from God by getting them to disobey God's command. Can you remember who that was?

He was crafty.

Read Genesis 3:1.

Now do you remember?

It was the serpent.

You have a being that is against God. You have a being that has been revealed to be a liar from the beginning.

Notice that he didn't even care what would happen to Adam and Eve.

He didn't even care that it would cause the fall of all mankind.

He didn't say, "Well, you will know the difference between good and evil, but keep in mind Eve, it also will cause you to lose your place here in paradise with God, and will cause the fall of mankind, so you better think it over."

He just outright lied.

He's like that all throughout history, but the worst example ever given that reveals the true nature of this serpent can be found in Job chapter 1. I'm going to wait till you turn to and read that whole chapter.

Go ahead...

I'm waiting...

Still waiting...

Did you read?

Did you read how Job lost everything in such a short time? How one messenger came with bad news only to be replaced a short time later by another with even worse news?

Now I want you to notice something. I want you to notice why Satan did what he did.

Was it because he hated Job?

Was it because he hated God?

Why did he ask to do it?

Wasn't it to prove God wrong?

Yes, it was to prove God wrong, and he didn't care what it would take.

It wasn't, "Sorry about this, Job, I really don't want to take anything or anyone away from you, but I have to prove something."

He didn't care!

Loved ones lost—he didn't care.

Personal property lost—he didn't care.

Pain in the body and heart of Job—he didn't care!

Now turn to the New Testament and read Matthew 4:1-11.

Go ahead...

I'm waiting...

Still waiting...

Did you read?

Jesus tempted by that old serpent; tempted to satisfy His hunger, tempted to test God with selfishness, tempted to be an idolater, tempted to turn His love away from God on to the devil.

He didn't care that Jesus was hungry.

He didn't care whether Jesus got hurt or not if He threw Himself down.

He didn't care about how much he had to give Jesus in order to get Him to bow down and worship him; the ultimate way of turning a love for God onto his own old serpent skin.

He didn't care!

Read of his brutality against this Jesus in Mark 15:16-20.

A crown of thorns that are over an inch long, like nails, pressed into His skull; the skull being very vascular streaming blood down his body; mocking Him by dressing Him in a purple robe, the color of royalty, falling on their knees in mockery before Him, striking Him on the head with a staff, pounding that crown of thorns ever so deeper into his skull, spitting on Him, then taking Him to be crucified.

Whip Him, mock Him, crucify Him: that old serpent didn't care!

There is only one thing Satan cares about.

"C'mon, Eve, take a bite."

Why?

"C'mon, Job, check out what is happening to you."

Why?

"C'mon, Jesus, give up, don't do Your Father's will."

Why?

It was all to spite God.

If you believe his lies, know for certain: Satan doesn't care about you.

You're not even important enough in his mind to even bother with—if it weren't to spite God.

It's all to spite God.

He wants to get back at God even more now.

Revelation 12:17 states that old dragon/serpent is enraged that he was beaten by Jesus, and knowing he can no longer hurt Jesus chooses to rage against those who obey God's commandments and hold to the testimony of Jesus.

"Why? Why would that enrage him?"

Don't you understand?

To obey God's commands is to what? ...is to love God.

He hates it when you love God.

He'll hit you with sickness and it doesn't even have to do with you—so don't flatter yourself.

He'll hit you with losing loved ones—and he's not even interested in you.

He'll cause someone in your family to die and it doesn't even have to do with you.

You think he's feeling victorious because you're crying? He's not even looking at you.

He's looking at God. "Aha!" he'll say to God. "How do you like that?"

He'll promise you the world then take it away at death, just so he can laugh in the face of God.

How does it feel that satan would make you think you have some value, just to snatch it away at death and be condemned with him? Just so he can laugh in the face of God and hurt God by stealing your soul?

He doesn't give two hoots about you.

We're pawns he uses to get at God.

How sick is that?

I thank God for Job.

I thank God for loving us enough to allow Job to be tested.

I thank God that He is all-knowing and knew Job would survive and not disown his God.

I thank God the book of Job was written.

It's the only book that unveils satan and shows him for what he really is.

The suffering Job underwent wasn't even in God's mind.

Turn to the final chapter of Job and read how God blesses him in the end.

It is vital that we understand the mind of God.

In the Old Testament Israel did some terrible things when they turned to other gods.

Remember what we looked at before, 1Samuel 15:23?

Rebellion is like the sin of consulting sorcerers or worshipping idols?

To worship an idol is the ultimate rebellion, whatever form it takes.

Look what Israel did when they turned their love to idols. Turn to and read these verses; Jeremiah 7:31; 19:5; 32:35.

There you will read of Israel burning their sons and daughters in fire as they worship idols; as they worship false gods called Baal; sacrificing their sons and daughters to Molech. You will note something of most importance in all those verses. Each time God states that such a thing was never a command from Him, nor did it even enter His Mind.

God can't even think up such things.

What do I mean, "He can't even think up such things?"

Wait ... first ... there's more:

You know those wicked murderers, thieves, and cold-blooded-psycho-war-mongers that you said you are not? Therefore you don't deserve punishment?

I take it then that you are glad that wicked murderers, thieves, and cold-blooded-psycho-war-mongers are getting what they deserve?

Read Ezekiel 18 verses 23 and 32, as well as chapter 33 and verse 11.

They will be punished, you will be glad, maybe even take pleasure in their punishment, but does God?

Well does He?

You don't know do you?

You didn't read the Scriptures I just gave did you?

That could be a revelation about YOUR love for God.

You don't want to take the time to read them.

You don't want to see things from His Perspective.

You need to read them.

Continuing now, according to those Scriptures above, does God take pleasure in such? No!

Why? 1John 1:5 states that God is Light, and in Him there is no darkness at all.

God can't think up detestable practices, because those are dark deeds.

God takes no pleasure in the death of the wicked, because taking pleasure in another's misery is darkness, and in Him there is no darkness at all.

Everything that you can see that is bad or in the very least, wrong, it cannot be from God.

"So then it's the devil! Satan! The devil made me do it!"

What a copout.

Let me share something else with you, just in case you ever think of flattering yourself by blaming the devil when you sin.

Read this passage in James then continue on; James 1:13-15.

It is your own evil desire that makes you sin; that makes you turn your love away from God and put it on yourself and others.

Search your New Testament and find out how many times Christ or His apostles ever state the devil makes you do evil.

He may set up stumbling blocks or things that appeal to the flesh, but we make the choice to be evil—like Satan.

"Whoa! Hold on! I'm not Satan!"

I didn't say we are Satan.

I said we're like Satan.

Isn't Satan evil?

Isn't God good?

Then if we're evil, who are we like?

"Yeah, but I'm not a cold-blooded murderer!"

Please. I know it's hard to grasp. But be humble, and try ...

Remember: by our own evil desire...

Whom do you want to be like?

You must choose.

Know this. To the devil we are cannon fodder; worthless pieces of meat.

He can lie to us; he has to.

It's the only way he can get us to turn our love from God.

He knows we don't belong to him.

We no more belong to him than the dirt under his feet; or should I say belly?

Plus, he can't make you his.

Not if I understand correctly what Christ reveals in Mark 3:27.

Christ is stronger. He bound Satan.

Plus if you love God, no one can ever change that relationship unless you choose to leave God's protective hand, for no one can snatch you out of the Father's hand, according to John 10:28-29.

But by lying, Satan can trick you into following his ways and so end up in hell because by so lying, he can train you into rebelling against God.

Everyone out there who doesn't listen to God is rebelling against God.

"What?"

Please. I'm not going to review again. Just flip back through the pages.

CHAPTER 5

CHRIST'S LOVE FOR GOD

"Ok, I flipped back. I reviewed. But then that means I'm a sinner. There's no way I can do everything exactly as God wants me to."

I agree with you. You and I are alike then, according to Romans 3:23, for there it states everyone has sinned.

"Yeah, but I'm constantly fighting with the same sinful desires. Even if I wanted to do exactly what God wants I couldn't because these desires are so strong."

Sounds like me, in fact, sounds like all those who have a love for God and therefore have His Spirit in them. The flesh does what is contrary to the Spirit, so there is a constant battle going on, according to Galatians 5:17.

"But you don't understand. I can't do everything exactly as He wants, therefore I'm no good. I hate myself. I'm wretched."

I have good news! It's there for you if you want to read it. Check out Romans 7:24-25. He wants to rescue you.

But you have to want to be rescued.

In order to want to be rescued you must see yourself as one who needs to be rescued.

I believe you're there right now. You feel hopeless. You need help. You need to be rescued.

Listen...

He came to take away your guilt.

Nothing or no one else can take away your guilt.

You can even go to church every day, you can do good works every day, but when you do something bad, you still feel guilty.

Let Him rescue you.

Hebrews 10:1-4 states even a law can't take away guilt. A law can only make you feel guilty when you violate it. It can't take away guilt.

Plus, guilt will not motivate. Guilt plays an endless loop in your mind that you are not worthy.

Here's a new loop offered by Christ.

Christ takes away sin. We are no longer guilty. In Him we are worthy.

Play that loop in your mind.

Is there a difference between feeling guilty and feeling sorry?

Sorrow brings about repentance, guilt does not. I may feel guilty that I got drunk and hit a child with my car killing them, but if I don't stop drinking and driving to make sure it doesn't happen again, am I really sorry? 2Corinthians 7:8-11 explains this quite well.

Guilt will not produce the kind of sorrow described in that passage.

Guilt will cause you to be depressed, mope; be negative.

God, in Christ, went to great lengths so we could become His people.

He went to great lengths to take away our sins, so as to remove our guilt so we could be a people of joy—

Excited!

Heaven bound!

Think on this; meditate on this…

> …He wants a relationship with you.

I repeat …

> …He wants a relationship with you.

You didn't ask Him.

You didn't even know.

He loves you!

Again …

> …He wants a relationship with you.

He went to great lengths to that end.

He became nothing.

He became a servant; a human being.

He even humbled Himself and became obedient to Death.

Read about this in Philippians 2:6–8.

Take special note where it states that He obeyed death. What does that mean?

Obedience signifies a choice. We have no choice when it comes to death. He became obedient to death (choice). Death wasn't forced on Him like us—He had no sin!

Not just any death, but one of humiliation…death on a cross!

So humiliating.

Naked.

Beaten and bruised and bloodied.

Like a common criminal.

Hanging on a cross.

While on that cross, according to Mark 15:34, He cried out to God, "Why have You forsaken Me?"

What was going through His Mind when He cried out these Words?

Would you like to know?

Do you really want to know?

Will you take the time to read it?

Turn to Psalm 22:1–18.

This Psalm was written approximately 1000 years before the crucifixion, yet it reveals to us the mind of Christ as He hung on the cross. It begins with the very phrase He uttered while on the cross, reveals the torture of being despised by the people, mocked, and insulted; of having His hands and feet pierced; His garments divided and gambled for.

Remember, He took the nature of a servant.

He became a servant.

He was made in human likeness.

Found in appearance as a man.

God became a man. That's what is stated in John 1:1, 14.

But there was one more characteristic He took on for us, one more thing that He became.

Turn to and read 2Corinthians 5:21.

He became sin.

He Who had no sin became sin in our place, to rescue us!

And then...

Then...

...the most brutal example of Divine Justice ever recorded took place.

The most violent expression of God's wrath and justice ever recorded took place—

In the crucifixion—

Of Jesus Christ.

He was not treated fairly.

He was not guilty of even one sin.

He was the only innocent Person Who ever lived.

Yet He suffered a cruel, horrible death.

Does that seem unjust to you?

Does that offend you?

Does that upset you?

It should.

Yes, it should.

Because—

You are responsible.

You ...

... and I.

God allowing the crucifixion of Jesus Christ is the most just and gracious act in history.

"But how can that be?"

What do you mean, how can that be?

"Well, He never sinned. He was innocent. So how can His crucifixion be justice and grace? That sounds diabolical to me. If God were behind it, then that would make Him diabolical."

That's true, very true, but you are forgetting about one thing.

Jesus voluntarily took upon Himself the sins of the whole world.

To that point He was innocent, but when He voluntarily took upon Himself the sins of all mankind, when He took upon Himself that concentrated load of sin—

To God He became—

Obscene.

An accursed thing.

The most repugnant thing that ever existed on earth.

God executed His wrath in total impartiality.

Do you see?

Or do you not want to?

God could not overlook sin, even when it touched His Son.

That's what Jesus did.

For you …

… and me.

Christ took God's wrath, the justice that was to fall on us.

He paid for it with His priceless life.

What's that?

Yes, it is sad, very sad. It would be—if it ended there.

He left His place in heaven.

He hung on a cross in humiliation.

He hung in our place, submitting to death, physically and spiritually, separated from God. The spiritual relationship He had with the Father for eons ended right at the cross. God turned from Him. Jesus called, but no One answered. Though He had no sin, death having no hold on Him, forsaken by God He cried out:

"Why have You forsaken Me?"

For the first time ever Christ understood what it was like to be separated spiritually from God.

From forever He had enjoyed an intimate spiritual relationship with God.

But now He was alone, forsaken by God.

God turned His back.

He had to.

Why?

Because the sins of the world were on Him.

The law stated, "You sin, you die."

Not only physical death, but spiritual...spiritual death is separation from God.

"My God, why have You forsaken Me?"

Heaven was silent...God turned away.

Yet He stayed, yes nailed, but He willfully stayed on the cross out of love for His Father. His Father knew exactly what had to be done in order to save the world. Christ knew exactly what had to be done out of love for His Father. A tremendous example of love for—

Sinners.

Ugly deniers.

Ugly deserters.

Liars.

You ...

… and I.

He died.

He was buried.

He went into Hades.

But wait…

He turned to death and stated He would submit no longer.

Remember?

He had no sin—not one.

He submitted willingly to death—death did not take Him!

Death had no hold on Him!

He had paid the price, not for Himself, but for us.

For you …

… and I.

He rose from the dead.

Now we can do likewise.

He gave His blood for us.

He paid the price required.

We are free in Him.

He came out of Hades as He said He would—the only One to do so.

He rose from the dead—the only One to do so.

He:

Lifted the deserters!

Lifted the deniers!

Lifted the liars!

Lifted all those who are sorry for their sins, those who repent …

Those … who have a love for God.

Lifted, and presented us as holy, radiant, without stain or blemish, blameless.

Now we can become His children.

He has rescued us, but we must respond.

One must grab the life preserver in order to be rescued.

The life preserver has a name…Jesus Christ.

So in the same way we would lift a life preserver over our head and around our body we must lift Christ over our head and around our body.

How?

We become a son and daughter when we are baptized into Him, for when we do so we are then clothed with Christ, so states Galatians 3:26-27.

This is of ultimate importance.

"Ultimate?"

Yes ultimate.

"Why?"

Think back...to our previous discussion concerning what it means to love God. Remember Jesus stated that He loved the Father by doing exactly everything He commanded? Remember that God is Light and there is no darkness in Him?

Because there is no darkness in Him, He cannot fellowship with us if there is even one sin in our lives. But if we are in Christ, if we are baptized into Him, if we have put Him on in baptism like a set of clothes, when God looks at us He sees Christ, not us. He sees a spirit covered in Christ who has done everything exactly as He has commanded...the only One to do so.

Wow!

He sees you loving Him perfectly.

He has become our righteousness, holiness, and redemption, 1Corinthians 1:30.

Outside of Christ we are lost, at the devil's mercy—and he does not even know what the word mercy means. It's not even in his vocabulary.

Remember the way God wants all to be saved and to come to a knowledge of the truth, 1Timothy 2:4.

He wants everyone to come to repentance, 2 Peter 3:9.

He demonstrated, in the cross, His love for us. How will you now demonstrate your love for God?

Remember, love for God is to obey His commands, 1 John 5:3.

Soooooo ... let us go over again what I have already stated, with some further explanation.

If it is your heart's desire to love the Lord with all your heart, mind, and soul, then it's necessary to obey His commands.

Now I thought that statement might come across to you as being unfeeling; like a robot. So I asked these questions.

When you show that you love your wife, or a best friend, or even your dad or mom, and do what they want to do, and it makes them happy, and you can tell it makes them happy, that there's no joy inside of you? That you're just like a robot, going through the motions?

Tell me, honestly. Do you want to love, or just be loved?

You see, the answers you are giving in your heart right now reveal whether you are selfish and only want to be loved, or if you are unselfish and want to love back. If you are selfish, when you are trying to love someone else and doing what they like, you will be like a robot.

But if you are unselfish and truly desire to make the other person happy, to really love the other person, then you will find joy in doing what they want because you know that's what makes them happy; you know it's for their good; not yours.

I also mentioned that we must be careful for there are people who will abuse that and say things like, "If you love me you'll do what I like," even if it's wrong. But you see? If you put love for God first, you can say to that person, "but we're both to love God first, and put our love for each other second, and what you're asking me to do puts you in first place because it's against God's commands, so no, I won't do that."

Remember? This is what is so great and unique about God wanting to be loved the way He reveals. Because even when He asks us to love Him by obeying His Commands, even that is to protect us. He created us. He knows what is best for us. He knows what will hurt us.

There are thieves out there. They'll tell you they love you, but they really want to steal your heart, mind, and soul for themselves. They don't want to love back, they just want to be loved.

That's why I asked, "Do you want to love, or just be loved?"

This is a very important question that must be answered if you truly desire to understand what it means to love; in the highest sense of the word. The answer you are giving, in your heart, even as you read that question, identifies where you are. Sometimes this can be a shocking self-revelation.

Because remember? If you only want to be loved, and don't want to take the time to love, then you are taking something without giving anything back, and that makes you a thief.

And so, if you're a thief, when you promise, "I'll always love you," to someone, it won't be sincere; so when you give them your love they will eventually find that what you promised was a lie and will end up feeling not only unloved but unfulfilled. This is where many relationships end up, with both people feeling unloved and unfulfilled.

The same can be applied to your relationship with God, with one difference.

When He asks you to love Him by obeying His commands, He's really saying love Him first so that you will find true love in your own life! If you put Him first, you will obey His Commands, which will protect you from the thieves, and you will have life and have it to the full!

Remember about the thief, John 10:10?

Remember, obey Me, which is to love Me; which is to protect you from those who say they love you, but don't?

Obedience to God is in fact Him still loving you!!!!!

You're obeying because you want to show Him you love Him, but He's asking you to obey because He knows the thieves are out there after your soul, and He wants you to obey so you'll be protected from them because He loves you!

He also knows that if you are outside of His Love, the best you can look forward to is an eternity without Him. And to have an eternity without God means an eternity without good. Just evil. For only God is good, and God is Light, in Him there is no darkness at all. So remove God and all you have left is darkness and evil...for an eternity.

But He will allow you that choice. Because to force you to love Him is not love.

Love can only be exercised by a willing heart.

And there are many people out there who have fallen in love with the thief. Christ referred to them as "lost sheep."

Let's make this part a little more personal this time by using a question.

Are you one of them?

If you are, even now, God loves you.

And He came to rescue you.

But you have to want to be rescued.

So use the rest of this book to learn how to love God. He already knows you and therefore loves you. Now you can learn how to love Him.

How do I mean?

King David once wrote that he had hidden God's Word in his heart so as not to sin against Him, Psalm 119:11.

Use the verses I ask you to memorize to write Scriptures upon your heart. This will make you confident in your faith knowing you have been equipped by the Holy Spirit through the Word of God. The Scriptures I put forward to memorize have not been chosen at random, but carefully selected as key to understanding how to love God. But memorize them because you want to increase your love for God, not as a religious work. Because if you feel that you MUST memorize the Scriptures I suggest, it will become tedious, no longer a joy. So look at the Scripture I give. Read what I have to say about it. If it seems to tug at your heart, in any way, then try to commit it to memory.

In the New Testament Paul wrote in 2Timothy 3:16 that all Scripture is from God. He wrote this to Timothy, who he was training to be an evangelist. Now we aren't all training to be evangelists, but what this reveals is that all the Scripture that had been delivered in the Old Testament, as well as the New Testament, was from God.

So use the weekly Scripture readings to take you through the whole Bible. If you read them all as I give them, you can read through the entire Bible in one year. But again, don't read them as a daily routine that you MUST do, for then it will become to you, a law. You will feel guilty if you miss a reading. You will try to catch up on missed readings. Eventually you will feel, because you missed a couple of days that you will never catch up, so you'll just stop doing any reading. No, that is not what they are intended to produce. Rather, they will be several chapters of suggested readings for each week. If you read them all, great! If you don't read every day, but just certain days when you have more time, great! Use them as suggestions for each week, so that, if one day you WANT to read from the Bible, you'll be able to look at the readings I suggest and just pick something out of them. Many times I want to read my Bible, but I don't know where to turn or where to start, so I read a verse here, a verse there, not really knowing what to read. Well, this schedule is designed for just that. You'll be able to look at what date it is, then look at my suggested readings, and have something to pick from! That promotes free choice! Read what you want, when you want! The suggested readings are not placed randomly, either. Some have been placed at certain times of the year so the readings will coincide with calendar dates, making them somewhat applicable to the day at hand. So let the readings be an opportunity to let God speak to you on a meaningful and regular basis, not a legalistic exercise which you MUST do each day. Readings such as those never get to the heart.

Then if you can find the time, apply the weekly focus exercises. They will spark your imagination to hopefully get you out and about; to get the creative juices flowing in order to promote a dynamic fellowship with other Christians; to stimulate your thinking toward making opportunities or an environment where you can make your Christianity a bit more "real."

Hopefully, all three combined, will help set you on a course where you will find yourself loving God the way He longs to be loved; not as one performing rituals or a legalistic set of rules, but having, as a natural part of your everyday life:

A Love for God

CHAPTER 6

PRACTICAL APPLICATION

A Love for God...hopefully, now that you have reached this part of the book, you have come to understand more clearly, just what that means. But now the question becomes, how can I put that understanding into practice? Well, if I said that someone had a love for me, what would that mean? Would it not mean that they knew me? That they knew what I liked? That they knew what I didn't like? Not only would they know what I liked and didn't like, but they would make sure that they did what I liked and did not do what I didn't like. I mean, if they only did what they liked, would that make me happy? If they spent their time doing things I didn't like, would I feel like they cared about me? No; of course not. The same would go for anyone I said I loved. If I only do things I like and did all the things the person I claimed to love didn't like, how could I then claim I loved them? I couldn't. Love goes both ways. So then, can I claim I love God if I don't know Him? Can I claim to love God by doing things I like, but have no idea as to whether He likes them or not? Can I claim to love God if I keep on doing things I like, but He doesn't like? Of course not; so together, let's try to communicate with God; let Him speak to us through His Word, and us to Him by the way we live our lives and through prayer. If we do this together, we should be able to understand what it means to have a genuine love for God.

JANUARY 1-7

So here are some verses I'm going to try to commit to memory this first week. The first week of the year can be a very busy time, but I'll try just the same.

John 1:1

Reading this verse is actually quite an astounding revelation, yet the wording is very simple. There is only one conclusion I can come to. Whoever, or whatever the Word is, that thing or person was with God in the beginning, and was God. I have found some Bibles that insert the word "a" in places throughout this verse to make the One Who is being referred to here "a God" instead of "God." But make no mistake, the Greek article that would signify the word "a" is not present. It reads just as it should. The Word was in the beginning, with God, and was God. So whoever this is referring to was and is God. I first came to realize there were thieves out there when I read this verse in their Bible and they had inserted the word "a". All trusted translations do not put the word "a" in front of the word God. I want to love God, not the thieves. I want to love God the way He longs to be loved, so I'm going to let Him communicate to me through His Words, untouched by others who want to confuse that message.

John 1:14

This verse really floors me! The one being referred to in the first verse took on flesh, lived amongst us, and came from the Father. Who could that be? Who came from the Father? Who took on flesh and came from the Father, full of grace and truth? Jesus Christ did. Again, this verse helps bring me out of the confusion created by the thieves. By remembering where this verse is I can refute those who make Jesus out to be just a good man or an angel. He, according to these two verses, was/is God in the flesh.

Now that I have some verses to commit to memory, a.k.a. write on my heart, I also want some verses I can just read. It's the start of the year so I want some readings that kind of apply to new beginnings. I'm also going to start with some readings out of the Psalms in the Old Testament. I like reading them before I pray. I also want a variety so I have something to choose from. Variety is the spice of life! Ok, I'm going to choose Psalm chapters 1-4 as good readings to do before I pray. To keep me in the "New Year frame of mind" I'm also going to set aside Revelation chapters 21-22. There Jesus reveals He is making everything new. Also 1John chapters 1-5 will be good. They speak a lot on loving others and what better way to start the New Year than loving others, or at least reading about it so that it's on my mind. Then I'm just going to throw some other chapters in that refer to "beginnings". Let's see, Genesis 1, John 1(different than 1John), Hebrews 1, and Colossians 1. There! That's enough variety. If I can't read each day, doesn't matter, as long as by the end of the week I finish them. But at least when I want to read, I've got some readings that are kind of applicable to the New Year. So all of them together are...

Revelation 21–22
Psalm 1-4;
Genesis 1
John 1
Hebrews 1
Colossians 1
1 John 1–5

Wow! What a great set of readings to start the New Year! I'll make sure to read Genesis 1. I really enjoy reading of the very beginning when God got into the creating mood. Just think, had He not, where would I be? I wouldn't! I'm also glad that He has a great imagination to spark that creativity! In Genesis 1:20-23 it records God creating all the fish of the sea, and the birds of the air. I only have to look at the variety in fish and birds to understand how "imaginative" God is. I'm going to do myself a favor sometime this week and visit a place where they display fish. Maybe I'll take the whole day just to go about to different places that have fish on display. There are so many colors, different shapes, eyes, and fins. Some are quite comical. I think some of the pet stores also have fish; as well as birds! Yeah, that's what I'm going to do. Just take some time to enjoy God's creations. It may turn out to be a refreshing way to start the New Year!

JANUARY 8-14

Colossians 1:18

I'm just going to try and memorize this one verse, if any. I want to remember that Jesus alone is the Head of the body. The body, of course, as defined right within this verse, is referring to the church. This will help me to refute those who claim that there is another head of the church that I must answer to, but no. The One Who was God in the beginning, the One Who took on flesh and lived for awhile amongst us, He, and only He, is Head of the body, the church.

You know? That's a really good verse for me to memorize. It makes it so much easier, rather than being confused by every person who in one way or another wants me to listen to their teaching. I can read the Bible, and I can understand it. I want to have a love for God from His perspective, not from mine or someone else. So I'll try and memorize that, but as well I'm going to read something that can make me wise in all areas of my life. I want to start my New Year with some wisdom, so I'm going to try and read Proverbs chapters 1-6. Job too. That's a book that is good for reading; another good book to start out the New Year. So I'll put Job chapters 1-9 down for reading also. Just one Psalm for this week; actually, not even a whole Psalm, but a small cluster of verses to read each time I pray, Psalm 119:169-176. Yeah, that'll do. So it'll be...

Psalm 119:169–176
Proverbs 1–6
Job 1–9

I mentioned above that Job is a good read. The reason I wrote that is because what he goes through is very relatable. Maybe not when it comes to the extreme of his suffering, for I have never been there, but when it comes to a lack of support from his friends. I mean, there have been times when people have doubted me without reason; it's not a good feeling. Job chapter 4, verses 3-5 really speaks out to me in regards to needing support, or being supportive. At times it doesn't take much to be supportive. I can think of several times when someone in my life has been a support to me. Often times it was just a kind word that helped me keep going. Sometimes support came in the form of an example set, and I would find strength to carry on. Many times this support was given to me by Christians who were pillars in the faith, and they didn't even know I was drawing on them for support. I often view these "pillars" as never having problems of their own, but like Job, even the strong at times can be dismayed. Job's friends just made matters worse. Everyone can use encouragement. Maybe it's time I invited someone out or into my home that has been supportive to me during my Christian walk. Perhaps someone, as I mentioned before, that doesn't even realize they were a support to me. Not sure what I'll do; perhaps have them over for supper; a dessert; or even just for a visit. Yeah, have them over and just let them know how they have helped me, and sincerely thank them. I know the way they encouraged me in the past always seemed to come just at the right time. Never know, a bit of encouragement in their direction might just be timely. After all, "pillars" never seem to let others know when they are down. Yeah, I'm going to do that; I'm going to refresh a "pillar".

JANUARY 15-21

Colossians 1:28–29

Ok, three verses to consider for memorizing this week. The first two are Colossians 1, verses 28-29. There is something very important being stated here. The apostles shouted out about Jesus. But there is more. They warned everyone they could to get into Christ so that they could be presented acceptable to God. In fact, Paul states that he worked tirelessly to that end. It must be important to be found in Christ.

Proverbs 16:25

Here's the third verse I'm going to try and memorize. It's so simple it's almost scary. I remember a time when I thought I had it all together. I felt as though I had a love for God. It pretty much went with the way I felt, in other words, it was a subjective love. So I felt I was well on my way to heaven. I had my own ideas about life and how to live it. It was even better, I think, than the standards of this world. Then one day I picked up a Bible. It became very clear to me, very quickly I might add; that my way of loving God was not His way. This verse made it very clear that though the way I had chosen seemed or "felt" right, it was not God's Way. If it wasn't God's Way, the sure result was death. I'm thankful He loved me and kept me to a day when He could show me how to have a love for Him that leads to Life…

For readings this week I'm going to stay in Proverbs and Job. Proverbs at times can get repetitive. Job gives me some drama. Inspired drama; frustrating at times. We have the big picture, just as God did. Job had no idea what was going on, so sometimes I don't like reading Job. With Proverbs along for the ride I can read some of each. It'll keep me balanced between logic and drama…so here's what I'll try to read this week.

Proverbs 7–14
Job 10–18

There's a verse in Proverbs 11 that states something about generosity being refreshing to others; Proverbs chapter 11, verse 25. Generosity is often attached to money. I find it easier to be generous with money than with my time and my hands. But I think when I use my time and hands the people receiving the "gift" usually appreciate it more. I'm going to get a digital camera, maybe borrow one, call up a couple friends, and spend the day with them. Go to a park; a mall; eat; visit some landmarks; and all the while I'm going to take pictures. I'll take some; they can take some; all on the one camera. But here's the best part that I won't tell them about. In the days after, I'll make a digital "photo-album", maybe in the form of a "slideshow", with added comments, save it to disk, then the next time I see them I'll give them a copy! Now that's generosity; with my time and hands! A generosity that will be cherished by all and long remembered...

JANUARY 22-28

Ephesians 4:4–6

Three verses this week; if I can. Sometimes it's good at least to remember the book, chapter, and verse; the reference. That way, even though I may not be able to quote it from memory, I can still find where it is in my Bible. But I'll try to do both. I'm pretty busy this week, so I won't feel bad if I can't. Hey! I'll never feel bad if I can't...the point being that I'm trying; just about got legalistic on myself there!

These verses in Ephesians make me uncomfortable; I want to believe there are many teachings from various teachers that can lead me to heaven; not just Christ's teachings. But that would be me wanting to turn the love from others onto myself. In other words, because I want them to like me, I wouldn't make such exclusive statements. Well, if I want to have a love for God, I need to understand that these are statements of exclusivity; there is one Lord. Christ shares that spot with no one else. I want to tell everyone there are many paths to heaven; many paths, same destination. But only because I believe that if I share this passage with them that reveals there is only one path, they may get angry with me and not like me anymore. But this passage states there is one path, one faith; that came from one Lord; as well as one baptism. If I ignore this passage, who am I ignoring? If I believe this passage and ignore my friends, then what? If I choose to love them more than God, what good is that? It's neither beneficial to them or myself. But what really makes me uncomfortable is this; if one Lord means one Lord, and one faith means one faith, and one baptism means one baptism, then what does one body mean? Is there only one church?

Let's move on...I know certain of my friends are not going to like these verses from Ephesians chapter 4. But if I have a love for God, I'll not let them convince me otherwise. Job didn't let his friends convince him otherwise. They thought he was a sinner because of all his sufferings. That must have been hard to not give in. I have let go of my integrity to please people. What I mean is; I have even agreed with others that I had done something wrong, even though I hadn't, just to get on their good side. I let go of my integrity; very sad. I recovered though, by the grace of God. Job never let go of his integrity, maybe even to the point where his vocal claims about his integrity made him bring God's Ways into question. Not sure, but all I do know is that when we get to the end of Job, God blesses him. So, I'll read Job again this week, chapters 19-30. I'll sprinkle Proverbs around in there as well and read chapters 15-20. So that's…

Job 19–30
Proverbs 15–20

Proverbs always sparks creativity within me; for instance, Proverbs chapter 18 and verse 16. I feel some creativity coming on…I'm going to go buy a gift; nothing extravagant, but yet something that shows some thought behind it. Perhaps I'll buy several "little" gifts, and store them for future use. What for? Now and then I visit friends. Now and then I get invited over to people's homes. I'm going to take one of these small gifts, sneak it into their home, and hide it somewhere in their house. I'll hide it where it won't be found right away; perhaps under some towels in their bathroom; wherever. I'm not going to put my name on it either…I like giving anonymously! How does that apply to Proverbs 18:16? If they don't know I gave it to them, how will they be able to open the way for me; or usher me into the presence of the great? I'm not sure they're supposed to…who do I know of that can open the way and usher me into the great? He saw me leave the gift…He knows!

JANUARY 29-FEBRUARY 4

Philippians 4:13–14

Two verses to write upon my heart this week. Philippians chapter 4, verses 13-14. I find these verses very encouraging. I understood them better within the context they are written after I read the preceding verses. It seems the Philippian church had stopped supporting Paul, and then had renewed their support. Although Paul is thankful for the renewed support, he makes it clear to the church of Christ at Philippi that with or without their support, he was still confident that he could do all he wanted through Christ; he made it very clear that the source of his strength was not in gifts from men, but in Christ. It is good to have other Christians in my life. Brothers and sisters in Christ should draw strength from one another. It is good to have Christian friends, Christian advice, and above all, Christian love. One way God desires to be loved is seeing me loving my brothers and sisters in the same way. But from these verses I learn that even if all those I know forsake me or are taken away, even if there comes a time when although I may be surrounded by brothers and sisters I still feel forsaken and all alone, I can know this: He is with me. Although brothers and sisters may help me from time to time, I must remember, I can do all things not through them, but through Him.

That's kind of a somber note, isn't it? Kind of sad that I might feel all alone, yet kind of confident building that I can know He is always with me. Job knew that. His friends sort of deserted him. In keeping with that thought I'm going to stay with the same two books for reading material this week. I'll read Proverbs 21-28, and Job 31-39, all the while reflecting on the verses I've memorized in Philippians. Maybe I'll change to something else next week, but for now I'll stay in Proverbs and Job. So that's...

Proverbs 21–28
Job 31–39

There's a verse in Proverbs 22 that brings back some memories; verse 6. When I first read this I understood it to mean that if I trained up my children in the way of God, that when they were older they'd naturally follow God. I found that quite interesting so I dug deeper into this verse only to come to the realization that the way it had been translated did not quite convey the whole meaning. I found that the way it is meant to be read is "train up a child in the way he should go and is going, and when he is older he will not depart from it". I understood now what God was communicating. It was also played out before me one day when I was spending some "fun" time with my two boys. I went out and bought some of that bubble stuff; the bottle of soap with the hoop inside that I would blow through to make bubbles go floating in the air. Then I sat down with my kids and I blew bubbles. It was fun!

But I noticed something.

My youngest son wanted to grab the hoop out of my hand and blow for himself. My oldest son just stood back and watched. He would chase the bubbles, blowing at them. The younger one would try to pop them by slapping his hands together.

They were different.

They were each unique "going" a different way, yet both needed to be guided to the way of the Lord, the way they should go, while they were still children. If I waited till they were older, it may be too little too late. Their minds were wide open, now! Yet each of them had their own way. It was up to me to watch them, pray for wisdom, and guide them to God, but both in their own particular way, so to allow them free expression. I couldn't train one and then use that as a template to raise the other. That would hinder their individualism and breed rebellion. They each will go their own way. It was up to me to bring God into that way while they were young, and allow them to develop their own individual faith. I thought deeply about this as they played with the bubbles; one laughing; one yelling; one pushing and shoving; one quietly watching; both different, yet both needing the same thing; direction; individual direction. I suddenly realized I had stopped blowing bubbles and was just sitting, staring straight ahead.

"Blow some bubbles!" my one boy yelled.

The other one just laughed and did a little twirl, excitedly waiting for some more bubbles.

So I did.

I just blew bubbles.

FEBRUARY 5-11

Colossians 2:11-12

I have found this verse to be very useful in my travels. It made something very clear to me. Well, it made several things very clear, but one in particular. I understood that according to this verse, God cut away my sins when I was baptized. So if I hadn't got baptized, my sins would not have been cut away. This verse didn't reveal that my sins had already been cut away by my faith, and now I was to get baptized to show my sins had been cut away. No. This verse made it very clear; God did a spiritual circumcision on me when I was baptized; at that point in time He cut my sins away. But that's not what impressed me the most. What impressed me the most was that these verses referred to this whole process as an act of faith; that everything was taking place; the circumcision of my sinful nature, not by human hands but by the hands of God; because of my faith in the power of God! So baptism is an act of faith! All I had to do was read it as God had communicated it. This is His Way of taking away my sins. To have a love for God is to find out His Way and obey it.

That is so cool! A lot is taking place at baptism! I don't see His Hands at work. I don't feel His Hands at work. I won't see my sins floating on the water; cut away. But nonetheless, I believe He has done so, based on what He has revealed; and that's faith! Wow! I need a change from my regular readings after that. Well, I'm so close to have read all of Job and Proverbs, so I'll finish up Job by reading chapters 40-42, but I'm only going to read chapters 29-30 in Proverbs. I want to save the final chapter in Proverbs for next week. I like to read it by itself, especially around this time of year. I want to add some feeling to my prayers, so I'm going to read a Psalm or two before I pray, so I'll reserve Psalm 5-6, and let's see, Psalm 55-56; just because they have similar numbers. But I'm also going to read a book I really like, and that's Jonah. It only has 4 chapters, and it's a good read. I also need to get into the New Testament so I'm going to try and read Ephesians chapters 1-6. And because it's getting close to Valentine Day, I'll read Song of Songs chapter 1-3, just to get my heart throbbing a bit. Now I must remember to not let these become readings I MUST do every day, but rather, just some references that I can choose from when I desire to throughout the week. I have some listings that I can go to when I choose, instead of just flipping through my Bible and reading whatever. So the choices this week will be…

Job 40–42
Psalm 5-6; 55-56
Jonah 1–4
Proverbs 29–30
Ephesians 1–6
Song of Songs 1–3

There's some verses in Ephesians chapter 1 that used to give me a head-ache; verses: 3-5. It mentions the idea of predestination. I misunderstood this for many years. I used to think that it meant God forced His Will on people. That He decided who is saved and who is not. Then one week something happened to me that made this all very clear. I had a lady that was very special in my life; well I actually had several; but one that was on a plane of her own. So I planned out two weeks in advance, a Saturday for her. Well, it was kind of for me too. I booked a massage, a manicure, a beauty make-up, a night at the movies, ending with an evening out for supper; prepaying for everything except the movie and dinner. Then I left her a phone message asking her to give me a call before the Satur-day which was a week in advance of the day I had planned. That's all I said, just for her to give me a call. Each day I checked my messages. I could hardly wait to tell her what she was in store for. What I had predes-tined for her and all she had to do was call me back on the phone. Well, the Saturday that she had to call me back on, the Saturday that was a week in advance of the actual day, came and went. My ego was totally deflated. So to pump it back up, I phoned another lady friend leaving the same message on her phone, except that she had to get back to me by Wednesday. She returned my call the same day! So I gave her what I had planned even BEFORE I had phoned her. Now I never told her I had planned it for someone else, but it made the meaning of predestination as used in this context very clear to me. The lady I had originally planned the day for had to call me. By her own free will, she had to choose to call me. Once she responded in the way I had chosen, she would receive what I had planned long before. Same with God; He chose, or predeter-mined, or predestined, that all those who choose to obey His Word, all those He would make holy and blameless in His sight. He planned this long ago, before the creation of the world. But He did not force it on whoever He chose; He chose to give it to those who exercise their free will. So I had planned that special day, and waited for the lady I had predestined to receive it. All she had to do was call me back before the week's end. She didn't call, so I didn't give it to her. I phoned someone else. Free will; the reward in Christ is predestined, but only to those who by free will choose to return God's call.

FEBRUARY 12-18

1 Thessalonians 2:8

Only one verse to memorize this week; one that reveals Paul's caring attitude; what he put first when it came to someone he wanted to share his life with: the Gospel of God. It's always best to put the horse before the cart. It's deceitful for me to pretend to be a friend for the purpose only of leading someone to Christ. It's one thing to already be a friend to someone, and then share my faith; it's another to pretend to be a friend hoping that friendship will win them to Christ. People can only be brought to Christ by Him working in me. So as Paul's example here, I need to share my faith, then delight to open my heart to them: Gospel first, friends second. Of course, does this mean that it's wrong for me to be friends with someone first and then share my faith? Of course not; but it is wrong, and rather hypocritical, for me to pretend to like someone just to get them to "church." Then after they become a Christian, I have little if anything to do with them because I really didn't like them that much to begin with. Then they abandon the Lord because they feel I "pretended" for one person only—myself. It would be good enough for me to share my faith with friends I already have. But in making new friends, perhaps let them know of my faith first.

Yeah, that sounds right. Well it's still Valentine week, so for readings this week I'm going to stay in a book that kind of deals with romantic matters of the heart, Song of Songs. I started this last week as I realized Valentine Day was approaching. So now that I'm in the actual week I'll read chapters 4-8. I'm also going to read Proverbs 31 this week for the same reason. Three Psalms will be good enough to keep me in the prayerful mood, Psalm 57-59, but I'm also going to try and read Philippians 1-4 and Colossians 2-4. Why not Colossians 1? Well, I save that chapter for the beginning of the year; it just kind of fits there better for me. Seeing as the verse I'm going to memorize is in 1Thessalonians, I'll read the 5 chapters that make up that letter as well as 2Thessalonians 1-3. Yeah, that seems good. So it'll be...

Song of Songs 4–8
Proverbs 31
Psalm 57-59
Philippians 1–4
Colossians 2–4
1 Thessalonians 1–5
2 Thessalonians 1–3

I was reading 1Thessalonians 2:8 getting ready to try and memorize it. I was having trouble concentrating so I decided to try that another day and so went into just reading 1Thessalonians 1-5. I came across the verses that reveal some information about the return of Christ and I just had to stop and meditate. The verses I'm writing about are verses 16-18 in 1Thessalonians chapter 4. It got me thinking to when I was a child and how I used to take the time to gaze at the clouds and just for fun look for images. The clouds are an amazing part of God's creation. Clouds were at times used by God, speaking through His prophets, to announce a coming judgment. In verses 16-18 of 1Thessalonians 4, Paul draws an amazing picture of the second coming of Christ. To think that whether I live or die before this happens, one day all those who have obeyed the Gospel will fly amongst the clouds. I meditated on this and when I thought of one aspect a chill ran through me. When I think on this passage I always imagine it being summer. What if it happened in the winter? Brrrrr! Anyways, this week I'm going to cultivate the child that is still in me. Whether it's overcast or sunny with a few clouds here and there, through my busy week, I'm going to take the time to sit back and look for shapes in the clouds. Who knows? I may be looking up at just the right time!

FEBRUARY 19-25

1 Thessalonians 2:13

Only one verse to try and memorize this week, and to top it all off, it's a verse that brings back exciting memories! Memories of studying the Bible with people and watching their eyes literally light up! I always rejoice in my heart when people open their eyes wide over a verse I show them that they had never realized before! I rejoice that God, not me, is opening their eyes through His Word. I rejoice and thank God silently in prayer when this happens; that they have received the Word as it actually is, God's Word, right out of the Bible. No creed from a man/woman. No statement of faith from a man/woman; simply—but oh so powerfully—God's Word.

Memorizing this verse and remembering that will spur me on to do some more reading. Let's see, what should I read? Well, seeing as recalling the experience I just wrote about has got me wanting to thank God even now, I'm going to spend this next week in the Psalms. Yeah, I'll read Psalm 60-62, and Psalm 95-97. I'll read one just before I pray. I'm also going to read 2Corinthians 1-9. Why 2Corinthians before 1Corinthians? Well, simply because I can! Sometimes it's good for me to read the answers before I read the questions. It gives me different insight than if I read them in order. Then, to see if what he teaches the men he is training to be evangelists would apply to the problems in the Corinthian church, I'll read the letters he wrote to the men he was training; 1Timothy 1-6; 2Timothy 1-4; and Titus 1-3. And, seeing as I'm on a roll, I might as well finish off by reading a letter Paul wrote to someone he knew quite well, Philemon. That should do for this week. So then it'll be...

Psalm 60-62; 95-97
1 Timothy 1–6
2 Timothy 1–4
Titus 1-3
Philemon
2 Corinthians 1–9

Once at assembly, when it came to the time of giving, I realized I had forgot to bring mine. I was disappointed, yet at the same time pleased. Why?

Because I realized I actually had something to forget. I mean, if I didn't give at all, how could I ever forget? Hilarious thought! Well in the readings I'm planning to do this week, there's a verse in 2Corinthians chapter 9 that I find very hilarious. It's verse 7, where Paul writes something to the effect...how does it go?...it's in the context of giving money...something like God wants us to give cheerfully? Now that's a command, that if I love God, I will keep. How could I ever possibly keep that command if I never plan to give? That thought is hilarious also! After further study of this passage I found out that the word cheerful as used here comes from a Greek word from which we actually get the word hilarious. So he's instructing the church at Corinth to give hilariously. The dictionary defines hilarious as "very amusing, extremely funny". So during the next week, I went out and bought a golf ball. I wanted to do something hilarious. You know those dimples on a golf ball? How many are there on one ball? Well I had no idea, so this is what I did. I took a guess, then taking a pen, counted all the dimples, marking them with a blue dot as I did, so that I wouldn't count any twice. I promised myself that the next Sunday when the collection came around I would put in my regular giving plus an extra 10 dollars for each dot I was out by my guess. Needless to say, my giving increased that Sunday! That was hilarious! Maybe next time I'll try to guess the number in a bag of jelly beans! Thinking back, I remember a time when I didn't give at all yet still felt I loved God with all my heart...hilarious!

FEBRUARY 26 - MARCH 4

1 Timothy 2:3–5

The passage that I'm going to try and memorize this week is quite straight-forward; perhaps more straightforward than I'd like it to be. Why? Because verse 5 "smacks" of exclusiveness. I don't like statements of exclusivity. They make the path narrow; perhaps narrower than I am ready to accept. I understand verse 4. I have no problem with that. In fact I really like that part. That is the very gracious part of this passage. It's what follows after in verse 5 that causes discomfort. The Truth being that there is only ONE way to God, and that is through Christ Jesus. That is an exclusive statement; No other religious leader can make the claim that he/she is any kind of mediator. What about a priest? Can't he mediate for me? What about a different prophet, can't he mediate for me? Does this mean that in the whole world, no matter where I live, if I want someone to act as a media-tor between myself and God that I MUST go through Christ? Well, yeah, that is what this passage is stating, and I didn't write the original. Paul did, as Inspired by God. God, through Paul, wrote there is only ONE. Christ Jesus. Wow! Can I accept that? Does it matter if I don't? Does what I feel or think change what is Truth?

This is making me uncomfortable so I think I'll move on. Get my mind off that and pick out some passages for reading. Let's see, I'm going to pick a different Psalm to read each day this week so I'll need 7; Psalm 98-104; that was easy enough. I should finish reading 2Corinthians so I'll read chapters 10-13. Then I'll read Hebrews chapters 2-13, again, leaving off chapter 1 as I like to read that chapter at the beginning of the year. To go along with Hebrews I'll read a similar book, James, chapters 1-5. So that's...

Psalm 98-104
2 Corinthians 10–13
Hebrews 2–13
James 1–5

There's a passage in Hebrews that I particularly like. It reveals something about encouragement; that we are to consider how to encourage. It's Hebrews 10:24. I'm going to do some considering right here on the spot...

let's see…I'm going to buy a blank card. I'm going to think of someone I'd like to encourage. I'll write on the inside of the blank card some encouraging points about this person. The next time I see them, I'll give the card. Hey! That wasn't hard, and will actually take very little effort, yet could encourage someone in a very special way. Perhaps I should consider ways to encourage more often.

MARCH 5-11

1 Timothy 4:1–3

Ok, another three verses to try and memorize this week, 1Timothy 4:1-3. In these verses Paul is warning the young man who he is training to be an evangelist, Timothy, that some would abandon the ONE faith.

In other words, it wouldn't bother them at all to introduce new teachings; such as, forbidding marriage, and commanding abstinence from certain foods.

I've heard of certain religious groups with such teachings.

According to these verses I'm not to be a part of them.

It's one thing to abstain from a certain food product because I believe it to be unhealthy. It is totally another to make it to be a command from God, when I know that God created all foods to be received with thanks-giving.

Just imagine.

If I teach people to stay away from certain foods as a command from God; or forbid them to marry as a command from God; I am defined, by these verses, as either being a liar or from the devil. Which one is better…a liar or a demon?

But wait, there's more!

If I am part of a group that teaches such, then I am following either liars or I am following a demon! Not much better.

I am to follow God, by accepting all foods with thanksgiving.

To follow any teaching that commands me to abstain from something God does not reveals that I am willing to love the teacher of that false doctrine more than God.

Wow! A good Scripture for me to memorize...

Now, what other verses can I just read for this next week?

Let me explain by what I mean by "just read".

The Scripture I mentioned above is one that I will memorize. I want to write it upon my heart.

The Scriptures I am going to list now are for readings alone during the week. The reason I will now list several for this upcoming week, is to give me a variety, so my daily readings will have flavor; or will give me a choice.

You see, I want to devote some time to God every day, but I don't want it to become a burden; a check list of works I HAVE to do. God doesn't want me to read His Word if it's something my heart does not want to do. Giving myself a choice actually makes my daily reading of the Scriptures something I WANT to do; which is what He wants. He doesn't want me to just go through the motions. Going through the motions will have no effect on my heart. Reading, and memorizing, and meditating on his Word because I have a choice, will eventually cultivate within me a desire to get into God's Word each day. If I read every day, but let's say, 3 of those days my heart wasn't in it and I just did it to check off that I had a Bible reading, it would have been better for me to just have read the Bible 4 days that week. Let's face it...those other 3 days I didn't want to...didn't retain anything...it was a chore...I maybe even detested having to do it.

That's why sometimes I may only have 6 readings in the Psalms for a week instead of 7. I like to read a Psalm sometimes before I pray to get me in the right frame of mind for prayer, but if I only have 6, that will give me one day of the week where I can choose to not read a Psalm. Or perhaps I'll be too busy and fall asleep before I read, or pray. It's ok! He doesn't want me going through a reading just to justify myself with a work oriented salvation. He'd rather I consciously decide to read His Word at a time when I can meditate and pray.

So I give myself several passages each week so that when I decide to sit back and read and pray, there are already readings listed so I don't have to waste time flipping through the Bible trying to decide what to read. It's fun! I also try and make the readings correspond to calendar events so that they seem somewhat applicable.

So here's what I'll do this week. I'll choose 6 Psalms again instead of seven, and pray one day without a Psalm to see if I've learned anything about prayer from reading the Psalms. What do I mean? Well, the Psalms are many times, prayers. I'll begin one prayer with my own psalm to God! If I miss a day where I don't pray, then I'll still have 6 Psalms to use for the other days! See what I do? It's a way to give me choice. It's a way to keep my Bible readings exciting! I read because I want to read, cultivated by choice, which eventually creates within me a desire to read and pray every day.

Here, let me make it clearer.

It's hard for me to exercise when I HAVE to. Yet if a group of us get together to play a game of volleyball, I WANT to! But it's still exercise!

So by allowing the freedom of choice, even if it means to miss a day, when I get to reading, it's because I do so by choice...not because I have to...and that makes all the difference.

So I'll TRY and read 6 Psalms this week; Psalm 105-110. I'll also read some wisdom from Solomon, Ecclesiastes 1-2. I'm also going to list the letters of 1 & 2Peter, as well as 2 & 3John, and Jude. These are all short letters, and grouping them together will give me a different flavor as to how each of these men viewed their walk with Christ.

See?

That's exciting!

I can hardly wait!

I might read all of those short letters in one day!

So that'll be...

Psalm 105-110
1 Peter 1-5
2 Peter 1-3
2 John
3 John
Jude
Ecclesiastes 1-2

That's exciting!

What's also exciting is that it's warming up!

One thing I like about a long cold snowy winter is that eventually, spring will come! I think it would be a good time to make spring come earlier regardless of the weather outside by buying someone some flowers. 1Peter 3:7 reads that husbands are to be considerate of their wives. He reveals that if husbands treat their wives as such, their prayers will come up before Him without hindrance.

Well, presently I don't have a wife.

But reading about the gracious gift of life Christ has given everyone who wants it creates in me the idea of new life...new life = spring...spring = flowers.

Maybe I'll cheer someone up this week by giving them some flowers.

If I had a wife, I'd give her some flowers, just for no reason in particular... just because I'd WANT to.

Sound familiar? ...WANT to? ...

MARCH 12-18

1 Timothy 4:16

This is a good verse for me to memorize. My lifestyle must reflect my doctrine. This is the kind of worship God desires.

There are two words in the Greek language that are used for the word worship. One is *proskuneo,* the other *latreuo. Proskuneo* is used of worship that God directs us to, such as taking the Lord's Supper, prayer and singing, following the pattern as commanded in the New Testament, etc. *Latreuo* is the way one lives out their daily life; not lying or cheating, being honest and good-willed, etc. Both words are translated as worship, but both are different kinds of worship that is given to God; and both are needed; life and doctrine.

This verse also states that if I watch both, I will save myself as well as those who may hear me. People are always listening and watching—perhaps from afar. Sometimes I may be speaking to a friend, and a bystander across the room is listening. Sometimes I may be speaking to a family member and a friend or neighbour is listening. They have heard what I believe in, but do I practice it? Am I for real? I have had members of my own family turn to Christ, but not until they watched me for ten or twenty years to see if it was just a passing phase or if I was for real. That's why it states to persevere, which denotes length of time. Christianity is not a speed-dash. It is a long, long walk. People who hear and who are watching may eventually join me on the path—if I persevere in my worship of God; both life and doctrine; *latreuo* and *proskuneo.*

To help me in this I try and read the Bible and pray each day. I encourage myself to this by having a variety of readings. I want the time to be meaningful, not read without comprehension. So my readings for this week will be to finish up Ecclesiastes. That is such a good book! I'll finish it up by reading chapters 3-12. I'll pick 4 Psalms, 7-10, to make sure I have at least 4 meditative prayers this week. Then I think it's time to get into the Minor Prophets. Spring is a time, at least where I live, when as the sun begins to warm things up, people are tempted to take things off. The Minor Prophets are good to get my mind where God's mind is, and review how Israel became immoral like the nations around them. God even mentions that they began to dress like the nations around them. This will help me with my life, the way I live. So I'll read the one page writing of Obadiah, the three chapters of Nahum, as well as the three chapters of Zephaniah... now there's a name for a child...NOT! Ha ha...so it'll be...

Ecclesiastes 3–12
Psalm 7-10
Obadiah
Nahum 1–3
Zephaniah 1–3

I mentioned earlier how Ecclesiastes is a good read. The wisdom contained in it, as it is written by Solomon, is truly jaw-dropping! Chapter 3:1-8 reminds me that there is a time for everything, and a season for every activity, and we need to take advantage when we still have the time! I was meditating on this and realized that I no longer take time for little things; important things; leisure time; even fun times together while I still have others. As I thought about this, prompted by this passage in Ecclesiastes, I realized that something had disappeared from the land. With all the video games and electronic gadgetry, I realized that I could not remember the last time I saw two people just throwing some hoops; playing catch; or setting up a badminton set, net and all. I laughed at the thought of playing a video game of table tennis a.k.a. ping pong, when it's not even that hard to set up a table and play a real game of ping pong. I need to cherish the real things, and not let such activities give way to technology. I mean what would I enjoy more? A simulated game of baseball with simulated men running on a big screen while I move buttons and joysticks; or getting out a couple gloves and a ball and playing catch with someone? One day I may not be able to even walk, let alone run. I need to enjoy the things that involve others whom I love while the time is right...meaning NOW!

MARCH 19-25

2 Timothy 2:15

Correctly handle God's Word. I'm going to memorize this one. I have made mistakes in the past simply because I did not handle God's Word correctly. How? Well, in the past I would apply passages that were written to Christians to non-Christians. I would find a passage that read "if you believe you will be saved" and instruct a non-Christian that all that was necessary for salvation was mental assent, not realizing I had just read a passage from a letter Paul had written to Christians instructing them how to maintain their salvation...not gain their salvation! I needed to learn and then handle God's Word properly. If I want to teach people how God reacts in different situations to the sin of man and show how God through-out all history has maintained His promise to bring the Christ to save mankind, I need to use the Old Testament. If I want to teach someone about Christ being the Son of God and God raising Him from the dead, I need to use the Gospels of Matthew, Mark, Luke, and John, because that is why they were written. If I want to teach someone how to become a Christian, I need to use the letter Luke wrote known as the book of Acts, because that is about the church starting and gives examples of what people did to become Christians. If I want to teach people in the church how to maintain a saving relationship with Christ after they have become Christians, I need to use the epistles of Paul, Peter, James, John, and Jude. If I want to teach people how to avoid using a system of works to maintain their faith, I need to use the letter written to the Hebrews. If I want to show people that no matter what kind of persecution arises, God is and will always be in control, I need to use the letter written to the persecuted church in the first century, Revelation. I need to handle the Word of Truth correctly.

It's kind of scary when I think that I could teach someone error by misapplication. I guess that's why the Scriptures warn that not everyone should presume to be a teacher of God's Word. That verse makes me want to get back into the New Testament, so my readings for this week will most certainly include the Gospel of John. I'll read chapters 2-21. Notice again that I don't include chapter 1. It is also one of the chapters that I reserve for the New Year. As well, I'll continue with a Minor Prophet and read Habakkuk chapters 1-3, another name for a newborn child! I'll round it all off with some Psalms to read before praying, Psalm 45-48. I think I'll also read Lamentations 1-5. It was written by Jeremiah and reveals how sad he was that Israel was falling...but also reveals that Jeremiah's tears are also God's tears. God never enjoys having to discipline those He loves, but because He loves...does so. Yeah, that'll be some good reading... good variety...so that's...

Habakkuk 1–3
Lamentations 1–5
Psalm 45-48
John 2–21

The last statement in the Gospel of John really makes my head twirl. No, not like I'm demon possessed. I mean, when I meditate on what it states, it makes me dizzy. It's chapter 21 and verse 25, the last verse in the Gospel. John writes that if all the things Jesus did were written down in a book, there wouldn't be enough room in the world for the amount of books that would be written. Wow! Quite a statement! I thought about that and wondered if he was exaggerating. Then I thought of all the books that have been written over time, from different authors, about Jesus. I thought about all the books that have been written by contemporary authors and all the books that will still be written...about Jesus. It's just never going to stop. But to get a better understanding of the thought John is trying to get across by making that statement, I believe a trip to a library is in store for me. I'm just going to browse through all the different books; go from aisle to aisle. Then I'll go to the computer where I can search for specific titles the library has and scroll...and scroll...and scroll...and scroll. Yeah, I'm really going to do that. Go to a library. Then this statement made by John will take on real meaning. And that'll be just one library. Then I'll sit down at a table, survey from my sitting position all the books and meditate on this passage again.

MARCH 26 – APRIL 1

2 Timothy 3:16–17

All Scripture is God-breathed. All prophecy, from both Old and New Covenants, is God-breathed. It may have been recorded by men, but it came by God. Therefore none of it can be set aside. That is why I am writing these Scriptures upon my heart…memorizing them. Sometimes the task seems daunting, but the more I do it, the easier it gets. I won't give up. I want to be able to teach other men and women, who in turn will write these Scriptures upon their hearts. I want to be able to refute false doctrine and rebuke those who teach false doctrine without shrinking back because I'll know without a doubt that I am standing on God's Word. Then I can correct and train other men and women, equipping them thoroughly for every good work. I won't give up. I will memorize these Scriptures. I will write these Words of God upon my heart. I am assured, that because of Him, I will never regret doing so.

Wow! I don't remember ever seeing myself so determined. I'm going to really get into the Psalms this week. I'm going to pick a Psalm for each day. I'll start and read Psalm 50-52 and end by reading Psalm 64-67. For the New Testament, I'm going to read through the Gospels. I'll start by reading the Gospels of Mark and Luke. But I won't read the first four chapters of each. I like to save those chapters for another time of year. So I'll read Mark chapters 5-16, and Luke chapters 5-20, leaving the last 4 chapters of Luke for next week to read alongside of Matthew. I just like having a choice, and if I read all of Luke this week, Matthew will be all by itself next week as it has 28 chapters. Perhaps it seems kind of silly, but it helps me keep my readings of the Bible varied. So that's…

Psalm 50-52
Psalm 64-67
Mark 5–16
Luke 5–20

Short and sweet; less varied this week, but the Psalms will help in that area. I don't know about your area, but it's snowing here. Yeah we get snow in March, but it's not very cold. In fact it's rather pleasant; snow-flakes lazily falling around me. Think I'll try and get out more. Maybe I could help my neighbor this week. Maybe shovel their walk, clean their yard, give them a ride; pick something up from the store for them, whatever. I don't have to look just next door. In my readings for this week comes Luke 10:25-37. Who is my neighbor? Surely I can find someone to do something for.

APRIL 2-8

2 Corinthians 5:17–18

What a beautiful reading! A new creation! What great verses to memo-rize! I will often meditate on these verses. I think of when God first created the entire universe and it was new. It had never been here before and was totally new. Like a newborn baby; fresh, unique, and new; all this from God, so that I in turn can share with others how they can become new. The old can be done away with, so that the new can come. Note however, that it is conditional: only if I am in Christ does God view me as a new creation.

For the regular readings this week I'm going to keep a Psalm for every day. I'll read the rest of Luke, and Matthew chapters 4-21. I'll save the first three chapters of Matthew for the same reason I saved the first chapters in Mark and Luke...for another time of the year. I'll save 7 chapters of Matthew for next week; reading the whole book would be just too much Matthew for one week. So that's...

Psalm 68, 82-87
Luke 21–24
Matthew 4–21

Yeah. Love the Psalms. They make me thirsty to read more of God's Word. I'll read a Psalm that praises God, use it to get me in a holy kind of setting in my mind then word a prayer of my own. The Psalms make me thirsty, and then further reading is like a cold cup of water to that thirst. A cup of water isn't much, unless I'm very thirsty. Then it's everything I've ever wanted! Jesus talks about how far a cup of water can go in Matthew 10:41-42. This week I'm going to look for someone who is thirsty. I don't mean physically thirsty, but spiritually; perhaps someone that seems a bit sad as of late; or someone who seems to be shunned by the majority; perhaps someone who has just experienced a severe trial of sorts, or even not so severe. I'm going to go out and buy them a small gift. Not anything expensive, something small. Get a card and write some encouraging words to them. Give them the gift and card. I know how much of a differ-ence a "cup of water" can make to me when I'm thirsty!

APRIL 9-15

Hebrews 4:12

One memory verse for this week, but it's one that brings back nightmares. Nightmares where I'm standing in the middle of a room with all my friends around and I don't have a stitch of clothing on! For some reason, in these dreams, no one else seems to notice but me, but I'm still very uncomfortable and want to run and hide, but my feet must get tangled up in the blankets for I find myself frozen, unable to move! I always wake up somewhat shaken after a dream like that.

God's Word, read or spoken, at times shakes me up. It goes right to my very core. Sometimes it agitates me; sometimes I even get a little angry, especially when I'm doing something wrong and someone quotes a Scripture to me. I don't mean someone quoting a Scripture just trying to annoy me, but quoting Scripture in a correcting way, in a loving and considerate way, but still in a way that leaves me feeling naked. I've done that myself to others; quoted Scripture to try and help someone get on track, not in a preachy offending way full of attitude, but as part of my conversation, referring to it as a way of life; but even then it still aggravates people, even though it's not the way I presented it. It's just because God's Word can penetrate deeply—very deeply; striking right at the heart.

So I want to memorize that verse quickly. The less time I spend on it the fewer nightmares I'll be reminded of! I'm also going to mix things up more this week. It's my birthday on the 10th. So it's sure to snow this week. I'm always given a bit of snow for my birthday...never fails! Yes, in April...every year! Ok, back to the readings for this week. I've been spending so much time in just the Gospels that I was beginning to find reading becoming a little tiring. So I'm going to give myself a present and spice things up! I'm going to keep reading Psalms. Maybe 88-94; then for no reason at all jump back and read Psalm 53 and 54. I'll read Matthew chapters 22-28 just to not leave that hanging, but then I'll switch to the first letter Paul wrote to the Corinthians. Think I'll read the whole thing; the whole 16 chapters. I've already read 2Corinthians, so it'll be good to read the first letter; the problem letter. Think I'll read 3 chapters in Galatians as well. I want lots of variety this week, after all; it's my birthday! There's another reason though. I started falling asleep a couple of times while I was reading last week. That signals that my readings are turning into a senseless ritual; a work to make me feel good about my relationship with God...wrong motive! So I'll try this variety, and make sure that if and when I read, I'm actually doing it because I want to...so...

Psalm 88-94; 53-54
Matthew 22–28
1 Corinthians 1–16
Galatians 1–3

I'll see how that works. Maybe I'll even skip a day this week, just to keep me having the right motive. Seeing as I'm on the topic of having the right motive, Matthew 23:11 reveals to me an area of my life that could use some fine tuning. First I'll have to find a "tuning fork". Let's see, what can I do; how can I challenge myself? I do pretty good preaching sermons; I do good teaching. I need something that'll challenge me in the area of serving. I know what I'll do; kind of simple actually, but rather daunting. I'm going to write out an I.O.U. of service, simple as that. Just write on a paper, "Need a room cleaned? Garage cleaned? A meal cooked? Need to get groceries? Grass cut? Snow shoveled? Yard cleaned? Well, here's your opportunity. I.O.U my personal time, please let me know the date you will require me." Then I'll find someone and give them the paper. That's it! I'll do it! Maybe I'll mention it's my birthday. Would that be fair?

APRIL 16-22

Hebrews 10:24–25

These verses are going into my memory because they bring back good memories...memories of handing out brochures for a special Gospel weekend! Memories of being spurred on by others to do such! Memories of a huge barbecue afterwards to all those who helped! I remember when I was young in my Christian walk I used to feel like people were bribing me to hand out brochures. But this Scripture reference put that thought on hold—permanently! These verses revealed to me that I am to consider, think up, look for ways I can encourage others. That barbecuing at the end was an encouragement to spur me on toward loving the lost! I am actually exhorted by these verses to think up ways, consider, how I may spur others on! The second verse reveals that I should not give up meeting together with the assembly. Now, it's right next to revealing I need to consider how to encourage, so the revelation of not to give up meeting together is not to be used in a discouraging way; making people feel guilty about missing Sunday assembly. That's not how this Scripture should be applied. The admonition is for my own good. It's good that it is attached to the encouragement verse, for when I assemble, I have the opportunity to encourage others! I'm going to try and spur others on through encouragement; not use guilt. I mean that would work for me as well! What would I rather hear; that I'm commanded to be here on Sunday, and if I'm not I'm sinning; or encouraged that I shouldn't get into the practice of missing assemblies because eventually it could lead to me giving up on them completely? I want to use the assembly as a means to encourage others toward loving each other and serving each other. The assembly should be encourage-ridden; not guilt-ridden...guilt does not, and will not, motivate.

On the topic of motivating, what can I select for daily readings this week? Let me see; well, because my memory verse has to do with encouraging maybe reading about how the first church was motivated will be good for this week. Acts chapters 1 to 24 should do. I'll save 4 chapters for next week. Another Minor Prophet would be good in the mix, Joel 1-3. Finishing Galatians by reading chapters 4-6 will fit as well. In fact, those chapters in Galatians will go along with reading the book of Acts because the letter written to the Galatians deals with the Christians there thinking about returning to parts of the Law of Moses, so comparing it to the church in the book of Acts, how it evolved, will help me to relate to the problems in Galatia. I'll also read six Psalms, 69-74. That should do it for this week. So it'll be...

Psalm 69-74
Galatians 4-6
Joel 1–3
Acts 1–24

Reading about the early church in the first couple of chapters of Acts is so cool. They were all so happy! Meeting daily in their homes; sharing everything with everyone who was becoming a Christian. Every time I read Acts 2:46 I can't help but smile. I'm going to try and do something with some brothers and sisters that'll make us all smile...maybe even laugh... perish the thought! What would be fun...or funny? Well, I'm a guy; I stand about 6 feet 2 inches. I'm fairly well built. I know! This should knock some of the macho guys for a loop! I'm going to invite a bunch over this week to help me bake some cookies; whether timid sisters or macho brothers. Pre-made not allowed...bake! And no one will be allowed to sit around while the "others" bake the cookies. Everyone gets involved. Yeah. I'm going to do it. Should be good for a laugh or two!

APRIL 23-29

Hebrews 10:26–27

Two verses for memorizing this week. In my early Christian walk I was witness to these verses being used to fill Christians with guilt and dread if they ever missed an assembly. I used to wonder if God, because I missed one assembly, quickly changed my relationship with Him as a friend to an enemy. It was upsetting to say the least. But if I have that understanding and use it to make people fearful of their salvation, is such method of motivation found in love? No, the motivation for that understanding can only be a desire to manipulate and control. These verses are much more than church attendance. They sum up what the writer of Hebrews has been writing about all along. Throughout the letter he has been admonishing them not to turn back to the Law of Moses, to the temple sacrifices. He has warned them not to turn back to the laws of circumcision. He has shown them how animal sacrifices could not remove guilt. He warns them here to not forget, that after they have received the knowledge of the Truth, the New Covenant, the sanctifying sacrifice of Christ that was given as a complete and thorough sacrifice once and for all time, that if they turn back to the Law, the Old Covenant, and deliberately forsake Christ and His church, no sacrifice is left for them. Salvation is found only in Christ. I won't find it in a system of law and works—or in "church" attendance. Yeah, that's what these verses are warning about. It'll be good for me to memorize them for two reasons. One, to remind myself not to turn my Christianity into a system of works; and two, to remind myself not to use this passage to scare people into coming to church. Does God want a bunch of scared people worshipping Him?

"Are you here because you have a love for God?"

"No. I'm here because I want to escape hell".

Doesn't seem right, does it?

Now, about other readings for the week...

Well, I'm going to have six Psalms again. You may have noticed a pattern; six Psalms instead of seven quite often. Why not seven to make sure

I pray every day of the week? For that very reason! I do not want to force myself into a position where I'm praying and reading just to keep up with a schedule. Don't I want to show God that I have a love for Him every day of the week? Yes I do. But does forcing myself to read some Scripture when I don't want to show that I have a love for Him? No. What it does is show that I want to love God the way I think. If I do a reading every day, then God has to love me because I filled my quota...my check-list; my work-oriented plan...my plan...not His! So this way I am constantly reminded of that, plus, it really does make the daily readings more enjoyable. I have something definite I can choose from; the Scriptures are varied for my many varied moods; and I can read them in any order! Choice equals freedom. I can even choose not to read! But actually, I seldom make that choice because the way I do the readings has cultivated a desire within me to read every day! I could go on and on about this, and already have, so let's see. Psalm 75-77 and then jump to Psalm 111-113. How's that? I'll finish up Acts just to tie it up as completed, so Acts 25-28. Romans is after Acts in the Bible so I'll just start into it as well and read, let's see; I don't want to make it too much, so Romans chapters 1-6 should do. As well, I'm going to go back to the beginning and start in on Genesis and read chapters 2-10. Notice again, I've left off chapter 1. I like to read chapter 1 of Genesis at the beginning of the year. If you check back you'll see I've already read chapter 1. By breaking the chapters up like this also encourages me to read because I don't want to leave loose ends, kind of; if you know what I mean. So then it'll be...

Psalm 75-77; 111-113
Acts 25–28
Romans 1–6
Genesis 2–10

There's a part in Genesis chapter 3, verses 7-9 that always causes me to meditate. It saddens me to think of how the Lord's walk was interrupted by the sin of woman then man. It reads that He was walking in the cool of the day, enjoying His creation, only to have it interrupted by the sin of Eve then Adam. I then reflect on the fact that ever since the creation has never been as it was originally. Today we have cars, busses, trucks, airplanes, trains... When is the last time I just went for a WALK. Yeah; A WALK! How does that work again? I use my legs and feet, and swing my arms at my side; one foot ahead of the other...it's coming back to me now. Now

I remember! A walk! I'm going to go for a 30 minute walk. Why? To help me more appreciate this passage. As I go along I'll take special note of God's creation as seen in the trees, the sky, flowers, grass, water; everything created to support and maintain a healthy environment for humans to live. Then I'll take note of humankind's creation. Buildings, skyscrapers, automobiles, roads, highways, polluted skies and water, paper and trash, most everything to destroy what God created. Everything God made was for me to enjoy; all at His expense, nothing for Him, except the joy of seeing me enjoying His creation. Everything that humans build is largely, if not totally, based on greed. "Our creation" doesn't even compare with God's. From the beginning and throughout history we have purposed to wreck it.

APRIL 30-MAY 6

Hebrews 13:7

Ok, two verses this week, but from different places. Same book though. Same chapter! This first one reminds me of the person who brought me to Christ. It also reminds me of when I first attended an assembly. I remember those who spoke God's Word to the assembly, and how that stirred my spirit. Even today there are those I look up to, who are helping me to maintain my walk with Christ. I wonder how they're doing. I need to get to know them better. I want to create and maintain a relationship with them so that if struggles arrive, we can be a source of encouragement to each other. Memorizing this verse will constantly remind me of that. The next verse kind of goes along with this idea, but there is a different aspect.

Hebrews 13:17

I've seen this verse used to corral congregations.

"See? You have to submit to me. I am a leader here, and the Bible says here that you must submit."

The same reasoning is often used when it comes to wives being commanded to submit to husbands. But the word submit denotes a voluntary action, not a forced action. In other words, I give my will over to them because they have shown that they love and care for me. It's the same reason I submit to Christ. God did not force my love for Him, He gave Himself and I willingly give myself to Him because of that. This is the same. So those two Scriptures kind of relate to each other, and they're fairly easy to commit to memory. Now, about daily readings for the week…

I'm going to continue with the same pattern when it comes to the Psalms. This week I'll read Psalm 78-80 and Psalm 114-116. For the rest I'll just continue with Romans and read chapters 7-16 finishing it, and Genesis chapters 11-18. Simpler this time; so that's…

Psalm 78-80; 114-116
Genesis 11–18
Romans 7–16

I'm going to do something this week that is really out of the ordinary. This idea has come to me after meditating on Romans 10:14-15. I'm going to go for a walk in a grave yard. I'll count as many of the graves as I can. I believe it'll help me relate to this passage, albeit in a very sad way. I'm hoping however, that it will bring things a little bit more into focus as to one of the major reasons I have been called to be a disciple of Christ. This passage makes some things very clear. How can people respond to this great invitation that I have received if they do not hear about it? Someone one day took the time to tell me about the Gospel of Christ. There are others who were blessed by being born into a Christian family. Becoming a disciple may then have been something taken for granted, always being surrounded by the church. What about those outside of the church? How can they call on God if they have not ever heard so as to believe? How can they hear if they have never been preached to? How many graves will there be when I finish counting? Out of those, how many of the inhabitants heard the Good News so they could believe and so be saved?

MAY 7-13

James 2:17

Another pattern!

Oh no!

What's happening?

Nothing!

Two verses again this week, same chapter again, and just a verse apart. I could memorize the three verses, but I don't want to so I won't. This verse reminds me that mental assent is not enough. To say I believe without any action equals a faith that is dead. The next one is even more to the point, albeit somewhat more graphic in its nature...

James 2:19

Even demons give mental assent. To say I believe in the one God without any action equals the faith of a demon. Ouch! Two verses to write on my heart!

Let's quickly move on to this week's readings! I'm going to just focus on Genesis this week and read chapters 19 to 35. Well, I'll keep some Psalms in there just to help me with my prayers, but only four this week. Psalm 117-118, and Psalm 120-121. Notice I left out Psalm 119. That's because it's humongous! I'll break that up into several readings for other weeks. So pretty simple this week...

Genesis 19–35
Psalm 117-118; 120-121

Please allow me to indulge in a little humor here. Genesis 22:1-19 is the first father and son picnic recorded. I hate to think of what/who the main course was. However, as I note in verse 5, Abraham was confident that the Lord would deliver Isaac, whether by raising him from the dead, or by stopping the sacrifice, for he states to his servant that they both would return after the sacrifice. Even later, when asked by a nervous Isaac where the sacrifice was, Abraham was confident in his answer that God would supply the lamb.

Abraham knew Isaac was the "Promised Child" through which all other nations would be blessed, and he was confident in God keeping His promise. Well, I may no longer have a wife at my side, but I do have two sons, and they live quite near me; time to plan a picnic sometime this week with them. If they don't want to, then I'll just plan a picnic for some other dads and their sons. I'll go all out. Actually have an open fire to cook hot dogs and hamburgers; or at least a barbecue, but an open fire would be more fun. Maybe I can get together with someone I know who has a fire pit on the property. I'll bring balls and some gloves, Frisbees, badminton set complete with a net and…enjoy! To think that I am one of those who are part of the "nations" blessed by God and fulfilled in Christ; the result of a promise made by God…at that first father and son picnic!

MAY 14-20

1 Peter 3:21

I need to memorize this verse so I can quote it to those who state that water baptism doesn't save. I need to listen to God. The relationship was severed because we/I/you didn't want to listen in the first place. If I listen to others and believe the opposite of this verse it will show I love those who teach baptism doesn't save more than God. To show I have a love for God, all I have to do is read this verse and listen to Him. According to this verse, just as sure as the water in Noah's day carried away the sinners and saved Noah and his family, so does water baptism take away my sins and save me.

That's an easy verse to memorize! Now for readings this week; I'm going to keep it simple again. I'll read Psalm 122-126; I'll use them before I pray which will take care of five days. I'll finish reading Genesis chapters 36 to 50, and start in on Exodus by reading chapters 1 to 5. So that's...

Psalm 122-126
Genesis 36–50
Exodus 1–5

I love Psalm 126. The way it is written makes me smile. Like men who dreamed, mouths filled with laughter that spilled out in songs of joy. That is how they felt when the Lord brought them out of captivity back to their homes.

I was held captive once...by sin that condemned and reigned over me. But now in Christ I am free. I remember when I got baptized and the joy I felt when I came up out of that water, believing by faith that all my sin was now gone. It was a great feeling. A feeling of freedom!

One day this week, perhaps after worship service, I'm going to invite some people into my home and bake a meal TOGETHER. I will not let anyone sit idle. We will bake together, eat together; and then reminisce about freedom in Christ. I will laugh...there will be joy! That joy will spill out as together we end it all with some songs of praise to God.

MAY 21-27

2 Peter 1:5–9

A longer Scripture to memorize this week, but it is one of my favorite passages. Eight attributes; or perhaps qualities are listed that kind of relate to one another as they go along. I can have a lot of knowledge about God, but without the aforementioned attributes, be as likeable as a dictionary. If I am not likeable, but critical of sin in others, forgetting that I myself was once the same, I will not be productive with that knowledge, neither in helping other Christians to grow nor leading others to Christ; a very humbling passage; one that I must commit to memory for my own good. Wow...please God, never let me become this way, critical of others who are in sin, forgetting that I once was the same...

Readings for this week will be six Psalms and some from the book of Exodus. I don't have much to say; still contemplating the message in that last passage. Want to get memorizing that one right away, so I'll keep this part down to just two books. Psalm 127-132, and Exodus chapters 6-22. That's it...

Psalm 127-132
Exodus 6–22

When I read Exodus 12:31-36, I can't help but wonder. These people had homes. Sure they plundered the Egyptians, but they left behind most all of their possessions. God was cleaning house. He was moving His people away from the dirt and drudgery of enslavement to freedom. The Israelites soon learned just how little they needed. How about me? Do I have old stuff lying in the garage, or basement; boxes I have never opened? Stuff that every time I think of doing something with it I suddenly feel tired? Why not clean house? Yeah! This week I'm going to set a day where I will go through all my old "junk" and either throw it out or give it away. I will find there is a lot of stuff I don't even need, or even forgot I had. Who knows? Maybe in the near future I will be called to uproot and serve in another field. I'll have less to carry! Less to move! Yeah! I'm going to clean house!

MAY 28-JUNE 3

2 Peter 1:20–21

This is an excellent passage to commit to memory. It basically instructs me to just read my Bible. To not give any passage my own "spin." Just as I wouldn't give a simple math equation my own "spin," I'm not to put my own interpretation on any Scripture (2+2 will always = 4 no matter how I "spin" it). The easiest understanding is usually the correct understanding. I need to keep this in mind and stay away from "spinny" teachers.

Which readings for this week? Same as last, I'll stay in Psalms and Exodus, reading Psalm 133-137, and Exodus chapters 23-36. That's it!

Exodus 23–36
Psalm 133-137

What a sad, sad feeling I get whenever I read the first four verses of Psalm 137. There's a song that has been written to these verses, and when I read these verses, Psalm 137:1-4, I hear its mournful notes in my head, which makes me even sadder. Imagine proud Israel, being led away into captivity by another nation because they had forsaken their God. Imagine their captors taunting them,

"C'mon! Sing us a song about how great your God is! Where is this great and powerful God? Our god is greater! C'mon now! Sing us one of your silly songs!"

How sad.

Sometimes during my Christian walk I made decisions that were not in accordance with God's Will. As a result things turned out bad and at times I was even taunted by unbelievers about my faith. Sometimes bad things happened that seemed as if there was no God even when I was still doing my best to be faithful, and the taunts would come. It had a way of stealing my joy. Making me feel sad, not even wanting to pray, let alone sing.

If the weather is good, I'm going to find the time to have a picnic this week, but by myself. I'll make sure the site is by a river, or at least a body of water; take my Bible, sit down close to the river/body of water, and read this passage thinking of all the times I have let God down. He has feelings; I have grieved Him; caused Him to cry; but never for Himself, always for me. When hard times come into my life, I must remain faithful. He will always turn it into something good…if not in this life, then in the next. I must not let those with taunts get me down. With God there is always a new day…a day of rejoicing. If I sin and suffer as a result, I need to repent, turn and pray to Him, and He will lift me up. If I am suffering because of the free will of others, I need to be patient, and wait for the Lord. He will deliver me. I'll sit for awhile by the river. Listen to the sounds. Look up at the sky. When all is said and done, He is still in control. I'm going to meditate on these things, right there and then. I need to always pray, no matter how I "feel". I must always turn to God.

JUNE 4-10

John 3:5

No one has, no one will ever enter the kingdom of heaven without being born of water and the Spirit. Two elements for me to keep in mind...water and Spirit. What better way for me to do that than by memory.

Which readings for this week? I'm going to have seven Psalms for this week. I want to have a special time of prayer after each of those Psalms. The last couple of weeks really have had an impact on me. What with the Scriptures I have been memorizing and meditating on. So I'm going to use Psalm 20-23 to help me get in a spiritual frame of mind for the first four days of this week. I like to take the Psalms and put my own circumstances in them, but use the prayerful words recorded to help me communicate my feelings to God. Then I carry on with my own prayer. It helps me a lot. The last three days of the week I'll use Psalm 138-140. I'll combine my prayers with readings from Exodus chapters 37-40 finishing that up then continue with Leviticus chapters 1-13. Yeah, that'll do it...

Psalm 20-23; 138-140
Exodus 37–40
Leviticus 1–13

I was just getting into an upbeat mood when I came across Psalm 139:1-16. Sometimes a great sadness overwhelms me when I read certain passages. It's not wrong to feel sad at times in reaction to God's Word. As a matter of fact, I believe it only right to have sad feelings in response to certain Scripture, as long as we don't dwell in it for too long. I meditated on this passage then suddenly thought of something very sad. God is everywhere. At first that pretty much summed up these verses in my mind. But on further meditation I discovered more. Where can I go that God is not? Even in the recesses of my mind; my thoughts; He is there. If I were allowed to be aboard the space shuttle, or even in the future should I ever have the opportunity to be on Mars...He is there! Should I find the deepest location beneath the waters of the earth, and be lowered down in a diving bell...He is there! Then a sobering thought came to mind. No matter how dark...no matter if all sunlight is shut out...why...even in the womb, before I was even formed, during that process, He is there! In fact, not only does He know the words that are upon my tongue before I speak them, He already knows all the days of my life before I live them! That was a sobering thought...but then something really hit me...

Some children have never had a birth day. No, I don't mean lived long enough to have a birthday, I mean they've never been born. They lived in the womb, but never were allowed to see life outside of the womb...

I'm going to invite some friends over to my house. Have a birthday cake; party decorations. Celebrate a birthday, but for no one present. This celebration COULD have been someone's birthday.

After everyone is gone, that night before I go to sleep, I will pray about this. I know there's only one thing that will stop me from being overwhelmed with sadness. I will think of these verses and be comforted with the thought that even in the womb, He was with the child, and is with the spirit of that child even now.

JUNE 11-17

John 8:31–32

Jesus makes a statement here, and the first thing I notice is to whom He is speaking. Yes, Jews—but more than that. Jews who believed Him! This is a great Scripture to memorize because it reveals that it takes more than mental assent to be a Christian. It reveals that I can believe, and not follow. Jesus is not talking to unbelieving Pharisees here. He's talking to Jews who are nodding their heads in agreement with Him. They believe Him. Yet He states they need to hold to His teachings in order to be His disciples.

Wow!

To think I can believe in Jesus yet not qualify as a disciple because I don't hold to His teachings!

Ok, let's see. I'm going to keep the readings simple again for this week. I'm going to read some Psalms but really mix them up. Psalm 11; 24-27; and 141! That ought to send all the legalistic-work-oriented-go-by-a-checklist-rejecting-God's-grace believers running for cover!

"What? You dare read God's Word out of order!"

Yeah, I do! But actually, I'm reading it in an order! I try to put certain Scriptures in an order that either is applicable to calendar dates, or I group things in a way that makes them applicable to each other. Or I just mix them up for fun! Cover your ears now…sometimes I skip a day.

Ok, enough.

I'll also read Leviticus chapters 14-27, and begin Numbers by reading chapters 1-7. So let's go over that again. It'll be…

Psalm 11; 24-27; 141
Leviticus 14–27
Numbers 1–7

Now I might not get to read all those references, but at least it gives me something to choose from rather than just idly pick a verse here…a verse there. Yeah, I realize they may be a bit mixed up, but just a bit. The readings aren't just idly picked either. They really do go well together.

I've been entirely in the Old Testament for awhile because I have been concentrating on what God expects of His people by reading of past experiences as recorded. I learn a lot that I can apply today. Not rules and regulations, but attitudes of the heart. For instance, Leviticus 19:32. Respect and love for the aged has diminished greatly. I'm going to make a concentrated effort to make a notable change from that in my life one day this week. This may require a bit of work, but it shows a great deal of love. I don't want to just visit someone elderly; I want to take them out for a bite to eat; for an ice cream; to a movie; whatever. One more thing… I'm going to make sure the person I spend time with is 65 years of age or older.

JUNE 18-24

John 12:48

Three verses this week to commit to memory. This first one; how important is it that I know the Scriptures? Why am I writing Scriptures upon my heart by memorizing them?

John 13:34–35

This passage I want to memorize because to me it is one of the greatest evangelistic statements in the Bible. Why do I consider it evangelistic? Because men will not know I am a disciple of Jesus unless they observe me loving my brothers and sisters in Christ. They can't observe me if I only practice this on Sundays, or at church Bible studies. It doesn't have to be applied to youth rallies or summer camps either. I can better apply these verses by inviting people I know in the world to go to a movie with some of my Christian friends so that they may observe me practicing my Christianity in a real-world environment. At Christmas or Thanksgiving, I can invite my Christian friends over, but also some neighbors, that again they may observe how I love my brothers and sisters in Christ! When I invite my friends who aren't Christians I can tell them not to bring anything, food or beverage—everything will be supplied. I'm not going to sit and fret before they come over as to how I can get them to study the Bible, or how I can approach them to invite them out to church; I'm just going to have fun and love my brothers and sisters, as well as them. They will notice something different. They will miss it after they leave. They will know that they were amongst His disciples, of which I am one, because of the love they observed we had for one another! Some will hunger and thirst long after for the atmosphere they experienced while at my place amongst my Christian brothers and sisters. Some will seek to have that thirst quenched, and that hunger filled. Plus they will know where I live and that they can approach me. After all, I had them over and welcomed them amongst my brothers and sisters in Christ.

That sounds exciting huh?

No?

There was a time I didn't think it was exciting either. I didn't know what I was missing...

Anyways, on to the Bible readings for this week; I'm keeping the pattern. Psalm 12-17; Numbers 8-24. In case you missed it...

Psalm 12-17
Numbers 8–24

Psalm 15:1-3 made me feel bad. I'm going to phone someone I know, but don't seem to get along too well with. Usually I don't get along with certain people when I haven't taken the time to know them. Yeah. A phone call is in order. Maybe even a visit.

JUNE 25-JULY 1

John 15:8

This verse that I want to memorize reminds me that I am a disciple of Christ. That doesn't mean I should put myself on arrogant display, but that I need to be amongst others so they can see this fruit that has become a part of me. This will also bring about opportunities to grow the other fruit in my life, souls to Christ!

John 17:22-23

The other two verses I want to memorize this week, to make a total of three, is this one in John 17. When there is no unity, there is disbelief. People all claiming to follow one Lord yet all practicing different teachings brings about division. Division was never in the heart of God or Jesus Christ. In the first century, it was one church and many gods. Today it is one God and many churches. Why? Division is in the heart of men and women who claim to follow God yet desire only to please themselves. According to these Scriptures, unity will bring about conversions to God. Now if unity brings about conversion to God, then disunity brings people to the opposite of God. God is light. The opposite of light is dark. Who is the one in darkness? He has a name.

Yikes!

I don't want to belong to a group that doesn't practice the teachings of God. Such a group brings disunity; such a group then is the opposite of light; such a group is led by the one in darkness...and I'm not talking about Darth Vader here...

Yikes again!

Let's get on to the readings for this week!

I'm going to keep reading in the order I have been from the Old Testament. I'll read 5 Psalms this week, but from different parts. Let's see; Psalm

18-19, and 28-30. I'll finish Numbers, reading chapters 25-36, and start into Deuteronomy reading chapters 1-11. There! So that's...

Numbers 25–36
Psalm 18-19; 28-30
Deuteronomy 1–11

Just getting into Deuteronomy this week and I find a passage that is particularly interesting. In Deuteronomy 11:1-7 God reminds Israel that it was not their children that saw all the great miracles. Why would God remind them of that? Could it be their children might take God for granted, not having any history of both the kindness AND severity of God? Might they eventually take this great Promised Land as a statement that God was with them no matter what and begin to go against His commands, forgetting of the severity of God and thinking only of the kindness? Time can cause callousness to the severity of God. Time when everything is good, the land is "fat", the wallet is "thick". History shows that having plenty usually results in moral decline. I believe my nation, Canada, is on the way down morally. Or is it just me looking through jaded glasses? I know one way I can find out. Sometime this week I'm going to a home for the elderly; just to sit down and visit with them; ask them about the morality of today and listen to hear whether or not it differs from the time of their youth; find out what effect they think the morality of today is having in the community/country/nation. Then before I shut my eyes in sleep that night, I'll read this passage again, and pray to God that He might put upon my heart a necessity to remember and tell others about both characteristics of God.

JULY 2-8

Mark 9:1

Two verses to memorize for this week, this one and the one below; both from the same Gospel, both from the same chapter. They are critical verses to memorize as one teaches about the time when Jesus would establish His Kingdom, and the other teaches about how the Law of Moses would soon be no more. About the kingdom, here in Mark 9:1, Jesus states that some who were with Him at that moment would not die before they saw the Kingdom of God. Say what? But what about people who are saying and teaching that Jesus' Kingdom hasn't come yet? Wouldn't that mean that there are some people still around today who haven't died, and they're waiting for the kingdom to come? Like, they'd be 2,000 and some years old! That is the exact conclusion I have to come to if I insist that Jesus did not set up His kingdom in the first century. He states right at the moment recorded here by Mark, who is Inspired by God's Holy Spirit, to people who were within earshot of Him, that some of them...yes some of those that were right there with Him right at that time...would not die before His Kingdom would be established. Wow! So that means, if Jesus is telling the Truth (and He states that He is), that if I teach today that Jesus' kingdom is yet to come, would I not be teaching falsely? I wouldn't be teaching what Jesus taught here, that's for certain, and He said it was the Truth. Jesus stated that some (plural) standing right there with Him would see the kingdom come with power before they died. Sure enough, in Acts 2, the kingdom did come, and with plenty of power!

Mark 9:7

Both these verses will be easy to memorize. This one, to me, is even more amazing than the one above! It sparks my imagination as I try to picture what went down here.

In the preceding verses of this one I'm going to memorize, Peter, James, and John looked up to see Jesus shining brighter than the brightest day. Not only that, but they saw Moses, as well as Elijah, standing their talking with Him. Wow! Moses was one of the greatest men in all Jewish history. The next was Elijah. Moses was the Lawgiver. Moses talked face to face with God. Moses came down from the mountain with the original Ten

Commandments written on stone tablets by the finger of God. And Elijah; the greatest prophet that ever was! To the Hebrews; which would include those presently witnessing this event, Peter, James, and John; Moses stood for the Law, and Elijah stood for all the rest of the communication given by God through His prophets. Elijah was the prophet of prophets.

Peter was at a loss for words. He wanted to express something, so he put Jesus on the same level as these other two great men, thinking that by doing so he was giving Jesus equal standing with them. He puts forth a plan of action which was to build three, sort of, monuments, in recognition of all three, one for Jesus, one for Moses, and one for Elijah. But God almost in answer to Peter's suggestion makes it very clear Who Jesus is, and that that they should listen to Him.

Say what? To the Hebrew mind such a statement by God would be overwhelming. The Hebrews listened to Moses. He was the Lawgiver. The Hebrews listened to Elijah. He stood for all prophesy as delivered by God through His prophets. Yet God did not say,

"Listen to Moses."

Nor did He say,

"Listen to Elijah."

No.

In times past, yes.

But there on the mountain, God declared it was His Son Whom He loved, and they were to listen to Him.

In other words, the Law was, but is soon to be no more.

The word of the prophets predicted, but soon would be fulfilled.

Peter thought to elevate Jesus to equal standing with Moses and Elijah.

God lifted Him above.

This was His Son Whom He loved. They were to listen only to Him.

Isn't that amazing? That will help me select the readings for this week. I'm going to read some of the writings of Moses, and only the writings of Moses. Even though they were important at the time he wrote them, God stated in the verse that I'm memorizing this week, well one of the verses, that they would be no more. They were to pass and Jesus was Who we are to listen to now that His Kingdom is. So I'm going to read Deuteronomy 12-31. But I'm going to mix some Psalms by David in there to help with my prayers, so I'll also include for the week Psalm 31-35. That'll be it!

Deuteronomy 12–31
Psalm 31-35

As I read the Psalm for this week, Psalm 34:3 really hit me...especially this particular verse. It's always fun to have some fellow Christians over and spend an evening together. I like being with people who I have so much in common with. There's no profanity, no gossip or slander. No stimulants other than a deep joy inside that I have in common with them, which comes from the Lord. I like when we share that together; and seeing as it should be shared, I'm going to invite some friends over to spend an evening with me; Christian friends. But that's not all. I'm going to invite an equal amount of friends/acquaintances over that aren't Christians. Now I realize some may say, or at least be thinking,

"Oh, but what if they bring booze?"

Huh?

What?

Well, then I'll tell them not to! I'll invite them over for a dinner. I'll invite them over for games. I'll invite them over just because I want to and tell them not to bring anything as I will supply everything. During this time of sharing with brothers and sisters and friends I will make sure a prayer is said that exalts God; perhaps the mealtime prayer of thanks. I want everyone there to know Who is important in my life! Sadly, and this reflects on my own failings, some of the friends I invite may not even have ever realized God is the most important One in my life.

JULY 9-15

Mark 16:16

This is probably one of the easiest verses to memorize, yet one that is most significant when it comes to salvation. I need this verse on my heart to defend Jesus' plan of salvation for everyone. I have had so many try to manipulate this verse. In every translation of the Bible I've ever read, including the original Greek, Jesus here states that a person must believe and be baptized to be saved. However, He states that a person need only not believe to be condemned. Now, does that read that because Jesus did not say a person that doesn't believe and is not baptized will be condemned, because He didn't mention baptism when it came to condemnation, because He only mentioned unbelief for condemnation, does that mean that I can then go back to the first part of the verse and state that therefore, only belief is necessary for salvation, leaving out the baptism part? Why does my head begin spinning when I listen to that logic? Perhaps it's not just dizziness but because I'm in the company of a demon who's trying to confuse me?

The Lord made an easy-to-understand statement, why should I make it confusing?

I need to listen to the One Who longs for me to love Him the way He wants to be loved, which is by me obeying His commands.

Salvation and condemnation are two different things. Jesus is discussing two different things here. He states what is necessary for salvation, and He states what is necessary for condemnation.

What does Jesus say is necessary for salvation?

Let's see, belief and baptism.

Now, what does He say is necessary for condemnation?

Not believing, so only unbelief is necessary for condemnation. One thing is only needed for condemnation. That's what Jesus states.

Now, what is necessary for salvation?

It seems to me Jesus mentioned two things: Belief and baptism.

Now, I want to get to the second verse I'm going to memorize this week.

Luke 19:10

Pretty easy to understand and pretty easy to memorize and...I need to go out and do likewise; straight and to the point.

Now, I need to pick some readings for this week. The readings in Deuteronomy, which I'm going to continue, will be kind of sad. Moses won't be allowed into the Promised Land. But that goes back to the first part of this book, remember? Where I used that example to help us understand God's perspective when we go against His commands? I need to keep that lesson close to my heart. I could miss out on tremendous blessings and opportunities by failing to love God as He longs to be loved. So I'll finish up Deuteronomy by reading chapters 32-34, and then continue on by reading Joshua 1-18. I want to see how Joshua does as leader of the Israelites. I hope he doesn't make the same mistake. I'll throw in some Psalms as well, four this week, Psalm 36-39. That should do...

Deuteronomy 32–34
Joshua 1–18
Psalm 36-39

I want to meditate on this sad episode in Moses' life. Especially as recorded in Deuteronomy 32:48-52, for God reminds Moses as to the reason for His decision. I've often thought of this time in Moses' life. To come so close, yet not enter. I shudder to think of heaven that way. I'd rather not see it at all than to see it and not be allowed to enter. But this is not speaking of heaven. This is an example of how serious God is when it comes to obeying His Word. Moses missed out on an exceptional blessing that could have been his. He still received heaven. But he missed out on what must have been one of the most anticipated rewards in his life. He viewed the Promised Land from afar, but could not partake of it. So here's what I've decided to do. I'm going to go to a mall. I'm going to make sure I have money to spend. I'll walk through the mall looking at the displays in the windows; if I see a great bargain, too bad. I cannot purchase anything this day.

No.

Today I shall be like Moses.

I can look, but I cannot go inside.

JULY 16-22

Matthew 7:21–23

To me, this is one of the saddest verses in the Bible and one of the most alarming as well. This is not directed at blatant sinners, idol worshippers, thieves, murderers, and the sexually immoral, although they certainly would be included. But if I read this correctly, it is directed at "religious" people; those who call Jesus their Lord, but do not do His will; those who call Him Lord, but do not make Him Lord. Imagine preaching to others about God, driving out demons, and performing great miracles in His name, even calling Him Lord as I do so, only to find out I have never been known by Christ. Let me correct that. He may have never known me in the past, but at the time being referenced here He will know me—but only as an evil doer. That terrifies me. I do not, on the judgment day, want to be referenced in this manner by Christ. To help me remember that, I'm going to memorize this passage, and try my very hardest to do His Will; which really boils down to having a love for God...obeying His commands.

Moving on, the passages for reading this week will be the same books as last, but I'll add Judges now that I'm coming to the end of Joshua. Plus I'll read 4 Psalms. So it'll be Psalm 40-43; Joshua 19-24; and Judges 1-16. That should be enough.

Psalm 40-43
Joshua 19–24
Judges 1–16

Why do nations/cultures always go backwards? Why do they not look around, see how their ancestors were blessed, take note of how they behaved, and follow their example? Why do they look back in history, and then jump off into immorality, and deceit, and all the things that are rotten, when they can see that the blessings their ancestors enjoyed came from living a righteous life before God? It just doesn't make sense to me. It seems, sort of, backwards, doesn't it? ...backwards thinking ... backwards...yeah. Aha! This will be fun. On my next day off, when I can just take my time, I'll start the day by reading Judges 2:10-15. Then, I'll go backwards...I mean it! I'm going to do it! For breakfast, I'll have supper. That's right; pork chops and potatoes and veggies. Or whatever I was planning to have that day for supper. For lunch, seeing as it will be the normal time for this meal anyways, I'll go out to a restaurant, but in keeping with the backwards theme I'll order dessert first, then the meal, then appetizers! That ought to give me some strange looks. If anyone asks me why I'm ordering backwards, I'll just tell them I'm being like my ancestors. If they ask further, well I may just have to explain. That should be interesting! Finally, for supper, at home, I'll have breakfast, perhaps pancakes; or bacon and eggs. Yeah, bacon and eggs! As I drift off to sleep that night with the aroma of bacon drifting through the house, I'll remember not to be backwards in life like the Israelites at times were.

JULY 23-29

Matthew 9:37–38

I want to be a worker in the harvest field but I want to be well-equipped. I guess anyone can go into the harvest field and anyone may glean a harvest, but those who are well equipped will glean much more. That is why I am memorizing these Scriptures. The confidence God will give me by His Spirit working through His Word will grow, now that it is being written upon my heart. How wonderful to be able to calmly, and respectfully, turn those who are seeking the Truth in the correct direction by pointing them to or reciting Scripture that has been written upon my heart. To calmly and lovingly rebuke those who are in error; to see the false teachers shrink back as they observe God's Holy Spirit working in me as I recite His Word, confounding them, and hopefully leading some to repentance. That is why I write these few passages upon my heart.

Ok, readings for the week; time to start giving more variety. I'm only going to read one Psalm, finish Judges, read Ruth, then get into 1Samuel. I'll read Psalm 44; Judges 17-21; Ruth 1-4; and 1Samuel 1-11. These books are all awesome. I love these books! So again it will be…

Psalm 44
Judges 17–21
Ruth 1–4
1 Samuel 1–11

There's a passage in this week's readings that really "wows" me! …1Samuel 3:1-11.The last person Samuel expected to hear calling his name was probably God. He so not expected it that it took three times before Eli finally figured it out, and when God called the fourth time, Samuel was ready to listen. I remember when I first became a Christian. My friends and family didn't understand this new direction I had taken, and it actually created enmity between us. It took awhile, but eventually they came to understand, and as a result, most of them became Christians. I wonder if there's someone else that was in my life long ago that our relationship became strained when I chose to follow Christ. Or maybe someone that I just kind of overlooked. I'll have to do some reminiscing.

Whoever I come up with it'll be someone that a phone call from me to them would be completely unexpected. Like God with Samuel. When I finally think of someone, I'll phone them…four times if I have to!

JULY 30 - AUGUST 5

Matthew 16:18

It's His church, one church, one Lord, built upon one confession, that He is the Christ, the Son of the living God. He is not stating that the church would be built upon Peter, but upon the confession Peter made, that He was the Christ, the Son of the living God. It is the Who behind the confession that is the Rock! A good verse for me to memorize to refute anyone who may teach that Peter is the rock Jesus built His church on; now to the daily readings...

I'm going to stick to one book this week; in fact, for the next several weeks. Why? Because I can! But also because this part of the Bible is a cool recording of some exciting events in the history of Israel; there's a lot for me to sink my teeth into, so I like to just read and meditate on it all. Real people, recorded serving God in a real time period, with real problems and struggles much like today. So I won't get tired as the book has enough variety of its own! So here it is; 1Samuel 12-31. Yep! That's it...

1 Samuel 12–31

1Samuel chapter 30! What a great chapter in the history of David! Plunder he had received from his enemies he was willing to share with those who did not help. He viewed it all as something to be shared. He was so thankful perhaps that God had spared him and his men those they loved, that he could not keep the plunder to himself. Same with my own "plunder". God blesses me whether I deserve it or not. Such is His great and abundant mercy. I've got something "fun" I want to do. Sort of share my "plunder". I'm going to either buy or make a gift. Who am I kidding? When it comes to this kind of thing all my talents can be found in the nearest mall. I'm going to go buy a gift. But something I have to put some thought into, something extraordinary; unique. Something that shows I have great "plunder". I realize there's no real significant "holiday" this time of year set aside for gift giving, but so what...I'll change that and make it a yearly thing! I want to splurge a bit. Not on myself. Whatever I buy I'll be giving to someone I know. But I'm not going to give so I'll be praised by those I give to. I want to create a scenario similar to David's. Now I can't go plunder someone, and there's no one I know who needs to be rescued...or is there? Maybe there's someone who could be rescued from the doldrums of summer. Now let me see, David actually had people that went with him to do the rescuing that did NOT want him to share the plunder with those that had not gone with him. Yet he did. So I'm going to try and find someone that I feel least deserves some plunder. Sometimes they turn out to be the ones that need it, as everyone else views them as having everything. Here's what I'll do. I'm going to park my car a ways away so it will not be seen. Then take the gift, put it on their doorstep, ring the doorbell, and run! I'll watch from a safe distance, hidden so they can't identify who I am, even dress in clothes I usually don't wear so they can't recognize me. I have a tendency to dress the same way all the time so they might recognize me by my clothing. When they see the gift they'll look around. I'll wave at them, then run, jump into my car that is around the corner and drive! I'm smiling now just thinking about it! It'll be great sharing plunder with those who don't expect it!

AUGUST 6-12

Matthew 28:18–20

All authority belongs to Christ. This is one of the last conversations Jesus had with His disciples. These are the last instructions He gave to His disciples. He did not tell them to go make disciples by getting people to pray Jesus into their hearts. He did not tell them to go make disciples by having people recite the "sinner's prayer." He did not tell them to go baptize infants; He told them to go to all nations and teach those who are teachable all things He commanded, baptizing them. Last words are special. These are Jesus' last words before He ascended. They are important. I need to memorize them.

As for readings, I'm moving on to 2Samuel, chapters 1-24. That's it...

2 Samuel 1–24

David certainly was talented when it came to writing. After all, he wrote and sang songs thoroughly enjoyed by God! In 2Samuel 23:1-5 he describes the one who follows God as being like the light of morning at sunrise. As the verse I'm memorizing this week from Matthew are the last words of Christ, so are these some of the last words of David as he reflected upon his relationship with God.

Not everything went well with David.

He lost the firstborn of Bathsheba, and later most of his immediate family fell to the sword, all because of his sin with her.

Yet one can tell from these last words that David never blamed God. He was aware of his sins and the consequences. With his last words he praises his God.

I'm going to try something very special. I'll write out some words of praise to God after some reflection on my life. Then on a day when it is possible; when I don't have to rush to work; I'm going to get up very early and go to a safe place where I can watch the sun rise. I won't stare directly at the sun. That would be foolish. But I'll look at the colors as the sun "comes up". It'll be beautiful! I'll meditate on the words David wrote about the one who follows God in these 5 verses I referred to earlier, then prayerfully read to God the words of praise I have written.

AUGUST 13-19

1 Corinthians 1:10

Religious division begins with religious people. They want to turn my love away from God to themselves. They are successful only if I turn from what I read in my Bible, God's Word; God's teaching; and turn to their teachings.

Thinking back to last week, I can recite, from memory, Matthew 28:18-20. It is so refreshing to have Scriptures written on my heart so that what I hear or read in the religious world, if it is different than the teachings of Jesus, can't turn my heart/love away from God. Because if Jesus told His disciples to teach everyone the same things He had given to them, every one of us who follow Christ should have the same teachings, that is, what we each read in the New Testament of the Bible, those are the things we should be doing. So we should end up with assemblies that agree with each other, at the very least, in doctrine. We might even have similarities in the way our worship is arranged.

The answer why this isn't happening can be found here, in this one verse I have chosen to memorize this week. If I base my beliefs on different concepts and ideas of people, I will undoubtedly, eventually, disagree with others, and because of those disagreements, eventually, separate myself from others. As a matter of fact, even now as I reflect on the many different denominations that are out there I come to realize this…any religious denomination would not exist without its doctrine. Take away its doctrine, and it ceases to exist; large or small. It is the same with the church of Christ. Take away the doctrine of Christ, and it ceases to exist. So if I want unity, I must turn away from all religious denominations that follow teachings outside of God's Word, and follow only the teachings of Christ that can be found in the New Testament pages of my Bible. I may state to people that I am with an assembly/church that belongs to Christ, but if I'm following teachings that do not belong to Christ, it is no longer His church. I then, with others, have gone above His authority, of which He has been given all, and established my own.

My appeal therefore, to others, must be the same as Paul's appeal to the Corinthian church that we all hold only to the teachings of Christ.

I'm so glad I'm memorizing these Scriptures...they are protecting me. By holding to them I am showing I have a love for God, and He in turn is demonstrating His love for me by protecting me, with the very Scriptures I am memorizing.

That is so comforting, and confident building. I am standing on solid ground. That is soooo reassuring. I can hardly wait to get into my Bible readings for this week; many examples that compare those who hold to God's Word against those who don't. I'm just going to stay in one book again this week. I'll read 1 Kings 1-17. That's it...

1 Kings 1–17

On the topic of holding to God's Word, and only God's Word, I meditate on this passage found at 1 Kings 17:1-6. Here I read about Elijah, a prophet holding to only God's Word, and suffering as a result.

As I thought deeply on this something practical about this whole situation came to mind.

I don't know, I'm a little squeamish when it comes to eating something someone else has taken a bite out of, let alone a bird.

Yet here is Elijah, being fed bread...and meat! ...delivered by birds?

Where did they get it?

All I know is to Elijah it was a feast. And, if I were in the same circumstances as Elijah, it would be to me as well. What I turn my mouth away from when there is plenty, I'd gladly receive if I was in want.

Think I'll go find some birds this week. Here where I live they can usually be found in parks or around fast food "restaurants". Prompted by these verses I'll take some bread, or muffins, or cake, whatever, and just feed the birds.

Watch them.

Enjoy them.

Think of Elijah and how grateful he must have been every time a raven arrived.

Notice the birds I'm feeding.

I wonder...?

AUGUST 20-26

Galatians 1:8–9

Here are two verses I want to burn into my heart. I mean...these verses... they...well...let me imagine.

I go for a walk one day and all of a sudden time freezes. I look up, and this glorious angel descends right in front of me, touches my forehead, passing on an incredible power, and in an instant puts from his/her mind into my own all the secrets of the universe as he/she understands them. Then with a glorious and angelic smile, while the sounds of other angels fill my ears, he/she nods toward me as if to affirm that all the things now in my heart are from God, and these new teachings are for me to pass on to others, starting a new church that would bring salvation to all.

What an incredible vision/experience!

What if the angel identified himself as the apostle Paul, or Moses, or David, or John?

What if she identified herself as Mary?

Could I resist?

Could I hold to the truths and warnings contained in the above Scripture?

That would be a very difficult temptation to resist, yet, God would expect me to.

Wow! I hope nothing like that ever happens to me. After meditating on that, and scaring the wits out of myself with my vivid imagination, I need to move on to what readings I'll do for this week.

I'll just continue in the order they're placed in the Bible. So that means I'll finish off 1Kings by reading chapters 18-22, and then start 2Kings and read chapters 1-11. Sweet and simple...

1 Kings 18-22
2 Kings 1–11

Sometimes I expect to find God where He is not. Sometimes I find Him where I'd least expect Him. I'm speaking spiritually of course. In my hustle and bustle life I rarely take time to look for Him. He is everywhere. All I need do is listen.

I'm going to try something that goes along with this thought that came to me while meditating on 1Kings 19:11-13. Maybe take some time to go for a walk where I can be by myself to just listen. Now I want to be serious about this. Perhaps a walk in a park will do. Or go for a drive and find a solitary place, as long as it's a safe place. As I walk, or as I sit, I'm going to listen and peel back the different layers of sound.

What do I mean by peel back the different layers?

If I'm in a park, at first I may hear people yelling or shouting as they spend time with ones they love. Listen to that, then peel it back, discard it, and listen deeper.

Perhaps I'll hear the sound of traffic on roads nearby. Keep peeling away.

Maybe a bird chirping here and there will suddenly come to the forefront that I hadn't noticed, or a dog barking, leaves rustling…concentrate, and peel.

Listen…carefully.

Quietly.

Peel back everything and concentrate, till I am listening only to the wind.

Now the hard part… I want to try and hear beyond the wind. I want to listen to…the silence.

Elijah.

All the wondrous and mighty things that were going on around him in an instant, yet God chose to speak to him with a gentle whisper.

Perhaps God has been trying to get my attention.

I need to take time to listen.

AUGUST 27–SEPTEMBER 2

1 Corinthians 16:1–2

Yes, they had a collection.

If I study Corinthians where Paul writes about the attitude necessary for giving, as well as the account of this collection in the book of Acts, I will find that although he commands the collection to be made on the first day of the week, expedient because that is when they would come together to partake of the Lord's Supper, it is not wholly speaking about the weekly collection that is done today. Today's collection has become more of a tradition of necessity than a command. It is used to pay the mortgage on a big impressive building, pay the power bills, heating bills, maintenance costs, as well as the salaries of the many on staff. This is not what this collection for God's people refers to.

The reference to God's people here is not directed at Christians in general. This collection was being gathered from the church for the Jewish Christians who were at present time undergoing a severe famine. That's why it is called the collection for God's people, as the Jews were often referred to as God's people, even after they became Christians, because of their long history as God's only people/nation.

This sets the pattern that I too then should follow. I should be giving to a collection on the first day of every week that will be saved up so that when a crisis takes place in another part of the world, there will already be money set aside to help, and no collection will have to be made.

Just a couple of verses that flow good together, so it shouldn't be hard to memorize them.

Now, on to the readings for this week; same as last week, I'm just going to continue in the order the books start and finish in the Bible.

I'll finish 2Kings by reading chapters 12-25 then continue on with 1Chronicles chapters 1-7.

I haven't had a problem for the last few weeks in finding the time to sit back and read the Bible. It's gotten to the point where I want to find the time, especially the stuff in these parts of the Bible. There's some overlapping of events, as some things are recorded twice, once in Kings, then again in Chronicles, but each time they're written a bit different, sort of a new perspective given on the same event. So then it'll be...

2 Kings 12–25
1 Chronicles 1–7

The reading of 2Kings 13:14-19 really teaches me a lesson. Elisha, in verse 18, instructs Jehoash king of Israel, to strike the ground. He does so, three times. Elisha then exclaims that he should have struck the ground five or six times, almost scolding the king of Israel! I've always found this to be a bit unfair of Elisha. Knowing myself, as little as I do, I would probably have said something back like,

"You told me to shoot only one arrow! I thought I was pushing things by striking the ground three times! Why didn't you say something? Had I known what you now just told me, I'd have struck the ground 100 times!"

To which Elisha probably would have sent a few bolts of lightning my way. I do have a habit of speaking out loud what I'm thinking inside, regardless of what the consequences might be.

However unfair I may think Elisha was being here, what this shows me is to never ask for a little when I need a lot. Never pretend to need less than what I do when I'm before God in prayer. Ask Him for what I really need. No point in "playing" humble before God. He knows everything I'm thinking!

I'm going to try something.

I'm going to have a party at my place.

First, I'll pray about it. I'll pray to God how I'd like to use this get together as a means of encouragement.

Then I'll invite both Christians and non-Christians.

Who knows?

Perhaps some of the non-Christians will enjoy themselves like never before. That could be the start of something interesting...to say the least.

Now...how many should I invite?

Three?

Four?

What's that thumping I hear on the ground?

SEPTEMBER 3-9

Galatians 3:26–27

How I'd love to put on Christ as I would put on a set of clothes. Wait a minute…I did! Note to self: this is another one of those verses that reveals how one gets "into" Christ. It's also connected with faith. It states that we are all people of God through faith in Christ Jesus because when we were baptized into Christ we had faith in Christ Jesus clothing us with Himself! Baptism is an act of faith. When God looks down at me, He will see not my sins, but Who I am wearing; great two verses to memorize. Easy too!

Now, what about readings for this week? I'm just going to carry on with 1Chronicles and read chapters 8-27. That is quite a chunk for the week, but I find Chronicles a good read. Once I get started I could just keep reading. But I'll hold myself back to these 20 chapters for this week. So that's…

1 Chronicles 8–27

1Chronicles 12:16-18 reminds me of how careful David had to be when he first became king. When he was running from Saul it was hard to tell who his friend was and who his enemy was. It's a sad statement when one has to fear his own brethren. But here David goes out to meet his Benjamite brethren, and gives them a choice…you can be a friend, or I will leave you in the Hands of my best Friend! David was confident; not only in that he had rid himself of any grudges against his brethren, but also in that God knew his heart and would judge accordingly, if the Benjamites were being deceitful. There are probably people I have put a strain on when it comes to relationships; some right from my own personal family; strained relationships that have stemmed as a result of my choice to follow God; some as a result of my personal family treating me badly, even though I was reaching out to them in love. It's time to let go of any grudges. It's time to trust God. He knows my heart…and theirs. I'm going to phone every member in my immediate family. I'll call…just to tell them…I love them. Not very macho…actually…that'll take a lot of macho!

SEPTEMBER 10-16

Acts 2:38

Two memory verses for this week, both found in Acts chapter 2, verse 38, and verse 42. This brings to my memory a previous verse I memorized back in the first or second week of June, John 3:5, the one where I took special note of two elements that Jesus had brought up—water and Spirit. Cool; it's on my heart; I memorized it and it's still there! Now, this verse that I'm going to memorize this week is a part of the first sermon preached in the New Testament Kingdom. Note the message of salvation. People are to be baptized, there's the element of water, and they will receive God's Holy Spirit, there's the element of Spirit! They are relative. The question now is; will I accept this teaching of Jesus, reaffirmed by Peter through God's Holy Spirit?

The kingdom had arrived. Peter delivered the first Gospel sermon. He had been given the keys and He was opening the gates. He commanded at that precise time thousands of people's attention. What an opportunity! Everyone in the audience is waiting anxiously, listening to Peter, waiting for instructions on what they must do to be saved.

Does he tell them to pray Jesus into their heart?

No.

Does he give them the sinner's prayer to recite?

No.

Does he wait for them to have an amazing religious experience to take place to prove they are acceptable candidates for salvation?

No.

He reveals to them the only way one can enter the kingdom of heaven. Repent, be baptized for the forgiveness of your sins, and receive the indwelling of Holy Spirit.

Clean the temple so God may indwell it!

Acts 2:42

The Greek word that is used here can be translated as, and is actually closer in meaning to, the word addicted. The people recorded here in this verse were addicted to the apostles' teaching.

This also brings to mind, which is so cool; having the Scriptures memorized, ready to be recalled; ah, sorry, this also brings to mind a prior Scripture I memorized Matthew 28:18-20. It seems they did just that. As a result the people, as revealed in this verse, were united as one. Why? Because no other men have come yet with their own take on what the apostles are teaching. No other men have come yet to confuse the Christians with their own concepts. It would be the same way today, but we have all these "spin-doctors" teaching their own ideas and making their own churches.

There's something happening to me.

Something very definitely is taking place in my heart and mind.

As I memorize these Scriptures, I've noticed a refreshing feeling—an eyes-wide-open feeling—a things becoming clearer feeling! A feeling that is a result of turning away from what I had previously been taught or what I had simply believed. As I write these Scriptures upon my heart I can't help but desire to learn more, to turn completely to the apostle's teachings only. No wonder things are becoming crystal clear; I'm moving out of fog!

This practice is becoming something I...I...crave!

Memorize, memorize, memorize!

Whew!

I need to calm down.

But it really is cool.

Okay. Okay. Settle down. Think...readings for this week.

What shall I have just for readings this week? Well, I need to finish 1Chronicles of course, so I'll read the last two chapters in that book, 28-29. Then I think I'll just continue and read 2Chronicles, all the way to chapter 15. So that's...

1 Chronicles 28–29
2 Chronicles 1–15

The first time I came across 1Chronicles 28:9-10 I was completely blown away. Not only does God know the motive behind any action, He knows the motive behind ANY THOUGHT; no wonder God cannot be mocked!

Thought: "I'll tell that brother/sister I love them just so they'll not stand against me, but I really don't even like them."

Uh oh...He knows!

I'm pretending to love for my own benefit.

Hmmmmm.

It's time for action; time to send someone I'm uncomfortable with a nice card...not for my benefit...but theirs.

It's also time for prayer; prayer before I even attempt this, so I'll do it with sincerity.

SEPTEMBER 17-23

Acts 4:12

Two verses to try and memorize for this week, both in Acts, one chapter 4:12, and two, chapter 5:29.

As I think of the first verse, Acts 4:12, I reflect on the great religious leaders that come to mind. I mean the great ones! I won't mention any names. If I understand this verse correctly, and it's not hard to understand, then, from this Scripture, all of those great religious leaders that come to mind are excluded when it comes to the saving of mankind.

There are not many lords; there is one Lord.

There are not many paths to salvation; there is one. It can be found only in the name of Christ.

Now for the second verse I'm going to memorize…

Acts 5:29

I'm going to meet many people during my lifetime, even some very important ones. I already have.

I've also read, or heard, of many great men, religious and otherwise.

Some were great philosophers.

Some were cruel dictators.

History shows the most atrocious were religious people who tried to force their own religious teachings on people, who, when they wouldn't submit, were tortured and killed;

"Psycho-spin-doctors."

But as in the past, so in the future, even to death, it is not men I am to obey over God; it is God I am to obey over men.

Moving on to the readings for this week, I'll just continue in 2Chronicles and read from chapter 16 all the way to chapter 36. So the readings are really simple for this week...

2 Chronicles 16–36

In this week's daily readings 2Chronicles chapter 25 intrigues me; it's about Amaziah. At first he receives favor from God. A man of God, a prophet, gives him the go-ahead to attack. So Amaziah does. He slaughters those of Seir, Edom, but then he thinks that he did it by his own might, and so instead of thanking God, he worships the idols he brought back with him as part of the plunder!

Duh!??!

What up with that!??!

So because of his actions, not because God just doesn't like him, for God does not show favoritism, but because Amaziah obviously doesn't love God, he is abandoned by God, which results in Amaziah being defeated by Jehoash. He wouldn't even listen to a prophet who prophesied he would lose because he had fallen from God's favor!

God is not whimsical, but humans sure are.

One moment Amaziah is inquiring of God, following instructions and winning; the next he is crediting himself for all his success, loving false gods, even threatening the true prophet of God...and losing!

What would cause him to do such a thing?

It seems Israel had a pattern of such.

Was it because they were the chosen ones of God?

Was it because they viewed their relationship with God as being iron-clad simply because of lineage?

I hope my lineage never does such a thing.

History shows that just because someone once followed God and even had a lineage that followed God it doesn't mean they'll necessarily continue to follow God as time progresses. "Lineages" have a way of using the lineage itself to prove Godliness, instead of whether or not they're still following God.

Well, to remind myself never to be like Amaziah, here's what I'm going to do.

I'm going to buy myself a thistle plant.

Do they sell those?

Well, if not, then a cactus...it surely has thistles...something ugly. That's right; an ugly thistle/cactus plant which I'll name Amaziah. I'll even put a little label on it bearing that name. Every time I check it to see how it's doing, I'll say,

"How are you this morning Amaziah...thirsty? You look kind of lonely."

When people ask me why I called it Amaziah, (or ask if I'm crazy) I'll refer them to this incident in Israel's history.

SEPTEMBER 24-30

Acts 8:18–19

This will be one of the most important passages for me to memorize. I love it. It explains thoroughly and completely how the gifts of Holy Spirit were passed on.

What did Simon notice?

He noticed only the apostles, in this case, Peter and John, could pass on the ability to work miracles.

Why would that be important to him?

Simply put, because that is how a magician then, and even in some instances today, made/make their money. You perfect an illusion, and then you sell the secret of how you did the illusion to another magician, giving him/her the knowledge to exact that same illusion. He/she in turn now has the right to sell the secret to another magician who might be interested; and on and on.

I think I can get a lot out of these verses and the surrounding ones. But if I just memorize these two verses, I'll know where to turn to in my Bible should the topic of miraculous gifts come up.

I think I'll scrutinize these verses, and the surrounding ones, a bit more.

If I read the verses prior to this, it is revealed that Philip is the one doing the miracles. Simon, was a magician. People followed him because he had amazed them with his magic.

Simon was a talented man.

But when the people saw the miracles coming from Philip, they were so amazed that they forgot all about Simon. They followed Philip around, and obeyed the teachings he was presenting to them which he had learned from the apostles, and they were getting baptized. It reads that even Simon believed and was baptized. Amazing!

Now Philip wants some of the people to experience the miraculous powers of Holy Spirit, but he can't pass that ability on. Perhaps there were so many people coming to be healed that he needed some help. So he sends for Peter and John who come all the way from Jerusalem to Samaria where he was, for them to lay their hands on people so that they could receive the miraculous ability to heal, which was the same way Philip received the ability. Because if I go back even further, I read in Acts 7, the apostles laid their hands on a group of individuals of which Philip was one, and from then on he could work miracles! Simon recognized this, and that is why he offers Peter and John money. He didn't offer Philip money because Philip could not pass on the ability to him, he could only do the miracles.

Just a minute now…let me think on this.

If Simon could be given the power not only to work miracles, but also pass that ability on, he could become very rich. He could go into a town, do some amazing miracles, and then sell the power by charging people for the "secret" to the amazing miracles he would be performing. And all he'd have to do is lay his hands on them!

Peter and John rebuke him for thinking that the gift of God could be bought.

This passage sheds volumes of light on a rather dark topic…the false-miracle workers of today.

First, there is an amazing difference between a false miracle and the real thing. The people, who at first thought Simon had the great power, were simply blown away by the real thing when Philip came along. I firmly believe I would've been too! It doesn't seem like the kind of miracles Philip was doing were like curing headaches. No! He's healing people who are blind, lame, or have other grave sicknesses and diseases!

I need to do some reasoning here.

If the ability to work a miracle could only be passed on by the apostles laying their hands on someone, as the text states Simon observed, then how do the miracle workers of today receive their power?

Are the apostles still going around laying their hands on people?

No. They've all passed on.

Does God give them the ability from heaven?

No. Because if that were so, why didn't God give some people the ability right there in Samaria where Philip was? Why did Philip have to send all the way to Jerusalem for Peter and John to walk all that way to Samaria in order to lay their hands on some people, so that others, there in Samaria, would have the ability to work miracles? It seems God had left that responsibility to Holy Spirit, but working through the laying on of only the apostles' hands.

Just a minute; let me check this again...

Ok, this is in the context of having the ability to pass on the power to work miracles. The apostles did not pass that on. They only passed on a gift, such as the ability to heal, or speak in tongues, which is other languages, or some other miraculous gift. But Holy Spirit did not work through anyone else to give these gifts other than the apostles. That is why Simon offered the apostles money, but not Philip. He didn't only want the power to heal; he wanted the power to give others the ability to heal.

I need to read this passage again. I mean not just these verses I'm memorizing, but the whole part about Philip and Simon the sorcerer. Be back in a few minutes...

Yep! It's right there. I'm not making this up.

So again; if the gift of being able to heal others could only be given by the laying on of the apostles' hands, what happens after the apostles all die? There would still be some that could work miracles, those who may still be remaining that the apostles had laid hands on, but they would not be able to pass on the ability, and eventually, they too would die, thus bringing about the cessation of miraculous powers resident in a man or woman.

Now this passage isn't referring to the power of praying to God to heal those who are sick. But it is directing my thoughts to that power being resident in a man or woman, who then would touch people who are sick, healing them.

I remember another passage now. Paul also writes about the cessation of these kinds of miracles in 1 Corinthians 13.

I've just had an unsettling thought.

The apostles have all died, so, needless to state, they can't lay their hands on people. But that's how the gifts were passed on. So then, where do people get the ability to work the miracles they claim to be working today?

God's Word isn't giving me a lot of room here.

Perhaps they're in the same line as Simon, the magician?

Brrr. I suddenly feel a chill in the air.

I'm going to move on and select my readings for this week. Let's see... excuse me...sorry...had to shake that chill off. I'm going to read all of Ezra, chapters 1-10, then start Nehemiah and read chapters 1-11. Yeah, that'll do. So it's...

Ezra 1–10
Nehemiah 1–11

Ezra is a great book. It is written about Israel's restoration. Chapter 10:1-4 made me take a second read.

At this point, things had almost been restored, however, perhaps not the hearts of the people, for in the preceding verses, Ezra prays for the remnant that is returning to the land asking God for mercy because of their present sinful condition. The men of Israel were still intermarried with women of other nations; the ones they had become worse than, the nations that had brought the wrath of God upon them to begin with. Ezra completely humbles himself. His example of remorse and bitterness of heart toward the sins of Israel commands attention. The people gather, realize their sinfulness, and desire to do what is necessary to make things right, which at that time would be no little task. They were willing to choose God over their own desires, no matter the consequences, because their hearts were stirred by the example of God working in Ezra.

Sometimes a sinful life, when corrected, hurts others involved. That is sad. Especially in this case with the men of Israel married to wives they're going to have to come away from in order to obey God under the Old Covenant.

Wow...that's heavy stuff.

From this example, if I'm trying to get an understanding on how to have a genuine love for God, I must love God first. If I love God first, there will be no sadness due to consequences of my sin to others involved.

What an example Ezra was to the people. He did not do this to draw attention to himself; his heart truly was torn, and he was responding as such.

There are people in Christ who I have met that have affected me in a GREAT POSITIVE way. I'm going to meditate on this for a while, then have someone from that group over to my home, for whatever reason. Then I'm going to let them know, face to face, just how thankful I am to God... for them.

OCTOBER 1-7

Acts 8:38

I'm only going to memorize one verse this week, but I'm also going to take special note of the context this verse is in. The one verse memorized will be enough as that will give me a reference point so I will know where to turn to if I want to share this with someone else. There's something here that blew me away!

It's about Philip again!

The verses prior to this state that the eunuch was reading Old Testament Scripture, Isaiah, and he asked Philip Whom it was talking about. Philip began with the very Scripture the eunuch was reading and shared with him about Jesus. Right after that, the eunuch ordered the chariot to stop because he saw some water, and asked why he couldn't be baptized.

Let me think about this...

It says that Philip told the eunuch about Jesus.

Now how on earth did the eunuch find out about water baptism seeing as Philip told only about Jesus?

Excuse me for a minute. I need to read it again...

Yep! I'm not assuming anything, and I didn't write this passage. Luke did. He records that Philip told the eunuch about Jesus.

The answer is quite apparent.

I can't preach Jesus without mentioning water baptism!

That is the only way the eunuch could come to that conclusion!

He is an important official, and he stops his chariot, goes down into the water, and is baptized by Philip, all in a response to Philip telling him about Jesus.

The eunuch wasn't told to pray Jesus into his heart.

The eunuch wasn't told to recite the sinner's prayer.

Philip didn't wait until the eunuch spoke in tongues or had some great miraculous experience.

The eunuch came to the conclusion he needed to be baptized in water, simply from Philip preaching Jesus.

Isn't that amazing?

God's Word is so revealing if I approach it as a little child. Just clear my mind of all preconceptions and read.

On the topic of reading, for this week I'm going to get back to a bit more variation. I'll finish Nehemiah and read chapters 12-13, then dig into Esther; love the book of Esther. Think I'll read the entire book at one sitting. But also, the verse I'm memorizing this week reminded me of my favorite book of the Old Testament. Plus, it's getting close to winter now, so I need a book I can curl up with in a big ol' comfy blanket. I'm meaning Isaiah, the one the eunuch was reading! It just happens to be my all-time Old Testament favorite! He writes so poetically, and through his prophetic words paints some very intriguing pictures! I can hardly wait. I'm going to get those other ones out of the way first! No disrespect to Nehemiah and Esther, but move on over and make way for Isaiah! Here we go...

Nehemiah 12–13
Esther 1–10
Isaiah 1–9

What a prophet Isaiah was. I have to take note of Isaiah 6:1-12.

Not all preachers of God's Word are recognized as great...especially when their message, from God's Word, is hard to swallow. Here God takes away Isaiah's sin, to give him confidence, to take a message to Israel. He is to preach this message until the cities are laid waste without any inhabitants, the houses vacated, fields destroyed, and the whole area left deserted. So it was...

"I don't want to go, for I am unworthy."

Then perhaps...

"Yikes! Now You have made me worthy, but the message...!"

Not all preachers preach God's Word in its entirety. Some preach it in a way to please the people in order to keep their "job". Come to think of it, I may know a preacher that stood up for what was right and it cost him dearly. He wasn't a very popular person then. I haven't seen him for a long, long, long time. A card is in store. I'll write in the card that I'm thankful that he stood up for what was Truth. I'm not going to email. I want it to have a personal touch. It's going snail mail.

OCTOBER 8-14

Acts 10:47–48

Two verses shouldn't be too hard.

These verses reveal what kind of baptism being baptized in the Name of Jesus is. They will also be good to memorize because once again, they are a reference to an important topic found in the verses prior.

In the verses prior to these, I read that the household of Cornelius was empowered the same way the apostles were on the Day of Pentecost. Charismatic religious leaders today run rampant with this, and teach all sorts of things. Well I'm not going to just take their word; I'm going to take a close look at this myself and come to an understanding free of preconceived concepts, whether taught or of my own. I'm going to read all of Chapter 10, so excuse me for a few minutes...

Ok, it's made very clear, from reading Acts 10, that God is trying to get the message to Peter to not call "unclean" what He has called/made clean. Peter is given a vision of a sheet filled with all the unclean animals he is familiar with, and told to go ahead and kill what he needs and eat. Peter states that he will surely not, for he had never eaten anything impure or unclean. The voice says that he is not to call anything unclean, or impure, which God has deemed to be clean and acceptable. This happens three times.

While Peter is pondering this new revelation, some men come who claim to have spoken with an angel who sent them to get Peter and bring him to visit Cornelius who is an "unclean" Gentile. Having just had the vision, Peter, the next day, goes with them. While in the presence of Cornelius and his household, Peter begins to share the Gospel message with them. As he begins, (Acts 11:15), the Holy Spirit empowers Cornelius and his household, Gentiles, to speak in tongues. So the ability to speak in tongues (which always means other languages) couldn't have been a sign they were saved because Peter had just begun to speak the Gospel. Yet even before they've heard the Gospel, as Peter hadn't spoken a Word of the Gospel yet, Holy Spirit empowered Cornelius and his household.

Putting this together with the vision and voice he had just seen and heard the day before, Peter comes to the conclusion that Gentiles, who were before unclean, were no longer to be viewed as such. It was God's way of showing Peter the devout Jew that Gentiles were to be included as prospects for the Kingdom as well.

Now, a question; is this the baptism of Holy Spirit taking place with Cornelius and his household? Or is it an empowering only? I'm going to compare the previous incident where the baptism of Holy Spirit took place with this incident. Back to Acts 2; again, excuse me while I read Acts 2:1-21…

Now, in Acts 2, there were tongues of fire and the sound of a mighty wind, though there was no wind, just the sound. That was the baptism of Holy Spirit, the pouring out of Holy Spirit. Then the apostles were empowered by Holy Spirit Who had been poured out, to speak in other languages, or "tongues." Peter again goes on to say that this was a fulfillment of what the prophet Joel predicted, in that God would pour out His Spirit to all mankind. Sorry, excuse me again for a few minutes. I want to look up that word "pour" in the Greek; be right back…

Ok, the word "pour" as used here means to completely empty, with none left over. So on the day of Pentecost, God completely poured out His Spirit, Holy Spirit, making Him available to all.

Now back to Acts 10. I note there are no tongues of fire, nor is there the sound of a mighty wind, so that is different than what took place when God poured out His Spirit, making Him available to all, as recorded in Acts 2. Here, Holy Spirit Who has already been poured out on the day of Pentecost, and is thus available to all, empowers Cornelius and his household, who were Gentiles, to speak in other languages, praising God.

Now I understand! That's why Peter was so surprised, because all other times the only way people could be empowered to work miracles was through the laying on of the apostles' hands. But here, God has made an exception, and through Holy Spirit He directly empowers Cornelius and his household, without Peter laying his hands on them. It was an exception.

Again, it was the only way God could make it clear to Peter and acceptable to the other Jews (Peter has to explain even going to a Gentile house in Acts 11) that Gentiles were also to be included as prospects for the kingdom. But this is an exception, and I should never take what God has made an exception and make it a general rule.

This empowering of Cornelius and his household to speak in other languages wasn't a sign they were saved as the empowering took place before they even heard the Gospel. It wasn't a "baptism of Holy Spirit" because not only were there no tongues of fire or the sound of a mighty wind, but Peter had explained in Acts 2 that the baptism of Holy Spirit, the complete pouring out of Holy Spirit, had taken place on the day of Pentecost. It was God making sure that His apostle understood that Gentiles were acceptable candidates for His Kingdom.

Peter tells them to do the same thing he told the thousands of Jews on the day of Pentecost in Acts 2 to do—get baptized! In so doing he also defines baptism in the name of Jesus as water baptism when he asks if anyone should stop them from being baptized in water, then, when there is no one vocally opposing this decision, he commands them to be baptized in the Name of Jesus.

So water baptism is baptism in the name of Jesus!

Amazing how it all just comes together! That's how it was in the first century, and how it can be now, as long as I follow only the apostles' teachings and not a bunch of "spin-doctors."

Spinny "spin-doctors" trying to turn my love away from God and on to them...not going to happen.

Ok, readings for this week! ISAIAH!!! Chapters 10-30! Might be quite a bit, but again, I love Isaiah. I'm going to get started...

Isaiah 10–30

I just have to mention this passage, Isaiah 10:5-19! The king of Assyria... used by God to discipline the people He loved, only powerful because God made him so. Yet the king of Assyria went too far. He became proud, and went beyond what God needed, thinking he had become so powerful in and of himself. And because Assyria went beyond what was necessary, and because he boasted in himself, because he took credit for all that he had conquered being a product of his own strength and might, God declared, in my own words, "stick a fork in Sennacherib, because as of this day he is done!" The description of Sennacherib's boasting, and the description God gives as to how he is going to bring Sennacherib low, as written by Isaiah is much better than my words.

Isaiah, Inspired by God, is amazing! That's why I love Isaiah. God truly shines as brought to light through Him using Isaiah's talents in writing.

I can hardly wait till next week to read what took place concerning this prophecy. But I won't read it this week...why? It creates within me a desire to read, and that's what I want. I believe that's what God wants as well; a desire to listen to Him as I read His Word; an excitement in my heart. Anything I can do to cultivate that in my heart I will do. So I need to wait...till next week.

Sennacherib became so haughty he became as dumb as an animal. No. Even an animal knows its master. He became dumber than an animal; as dumb as a stuffed animal. What a tragedy in the life of Sennacherib, king of Assyria.

I'm going to buy a stuffed animal. A donkey if I can find one. Put a little name tag around its neck, "Sennacherib". This will always remind me not to go too far in judging anyone harshly before God. God may use me to correct someone in His Body. If and when He does, I want something in my home that will always remind me not to become proud like Sennacherib did.

OCTOBER 15-21

Acts 20:7

Two verses for memorizing this week; verse 7 of Acts 20, and the one below, verse 16 of Acts 22.

Ok, the first one, Acts 20:7. The early church assembled on the first day of the week.

Is church assembly important?

Yes, because the church breaks bread together on the first day of the week. This is part of the apostles' teaching. It is a communion that the church is to take together, identifying with one another that they as a group, belong to each other, forming Christ's body. In fact, Paul actually waits a few days, even though he is in a hurry to move on, because he knew the church would assemble on the first day of the week to partake of the Lord's Supper.

Now some may try to confuse the issue and say that the first day of the week to the Jewish mind actually begins on our Saturday late afternoon/ evening. Using that logic the claim is then made that the church as recorded here, were actually meeting on Saturday, so we as Christians should worship on the seventh day.

Well, let me use some logic.

Luke is a Gentile, has a Gentile mind, and he's writing to Theophilus who is also a Gentile, with a Gentile mind. I'm not guessing at this. I read that in the opening verses of this book. Now, if I, with a Gentile mind, am communicating to a Gentile mind, and I wanted to tell him about something that happened on the first day of the week, how would I communicate that? I would probably say,

"On the first day of the week..."

Which we would both understand as...

"The first day of the week"!

If his first day of the week was Sunday, then it would mean Sunday.

If someone wants to insist this took place on Saturday night to justify their Old Covenant "spin" on things, then they have to at least admit, that even by their own interpretation, it couldn't then take place on the seventh day. Because, even according to their rules, the seventh day to the Jewish Old Covenant mind ended Saturday night and the first day of the week began. So even by their own Old Covenant "spin" on things, this took place on Saturday night, and therefore, would still, to the Jewish Old Covenant mind, be the first day of the week and not the seventh day. So no matter how you look at it, Paul broke bread with these people on the first day of the week.

Now, my first day of the week is Sunday. So when the first day of the week arrives, I try to find some Christians to assemble with so I can partake of the Lord's Supper with them. After all, I am supposed to devote myself to the apostles' New Covenant teachings, remember?

Acts 22:16

This second verse I'm memorizing is in the context of Paul's discourse to the mob at Jerusalem. He mentioned how He saw a bright light and actually talked with the Lord Jesus Who identified Himself to Paul and then told him to go to Ananias for further instructions. Upon reaching this destination, Ananias tells Paul that God has chosen him to actually hear Words from His mouth, to see the Righteous One, and then witness everything he saw and heard to all nations. Ananias further instructs Paul to not hesitate, but to be baptized so that his sins could be washed away.

Let me get this straight.

Paul had quite an experience here.

Paul sees a bright flash in the middle of a bright day. So the flash had to be from God, as it outshone the brightest of days. Surely God giving him such a sign meant he was saved. Then he actually converses with Jesus, Who identifies Himself to Paul, and Paul calls Him Lord showing reverence if not repentance. Surely now that he has seen a miraculous sign and actually talked to Jesus, he must be saved. Yet can a man be saved in his sins? Such a statement is ludicrous. Salvation means to be saved from your sins. Yet even after these great miraculous signs, Ananias reveals to Paul that his sins have yet to be forgiven when he commands Paul to hesitate no more, but to rise up and be baptized to have his sins washed away.

How then do I wash my sins away?

Ananias was just another Christian who had devoted himself to the apostles' teachings who had been taught by Christ.

My sins need to be washed away by doing as commanded according to the teachings of Christ and His apostles. There is no other way. The questions now are; do I have faith in Christ and the teachings of His apostles? Do I have a love for God?

Yeah I do and I did and my sins have been washed away. What a deep calm. To know, not subjectively, that is, by feelings, but to know objectively because I believe in what has been written by God, that my sins have been washed away. Amen!

What are my readings for this week? None other than good ol' Isaiah!

Isaiah 31–51

My attention was caught while doing the readings for this week by Isaiah 40:21-31. Just an amazing passage of Scripture; little hints all throughout that it is most definitely from God and not man.

As I read Isaiah, I find much of it depicts what is to happen years before it does.

Assyria to discipline Israel by God's Hand; then Babylon; and finally He even mentions by name, Cyrus, the king of the Mede/Persian empire; all sent by His Hand to discipline Israel and turn them from idolatry, to the One and only True God.

In verse 22 of this amazing passage the earth is described as being round when man still believed the earth to be flat, at least amongst the Gentile nations. Over and over again He takes credit for the creation of all things, and then He asks Israel for the reasoning behind the question of why they would think that He has forgotten about them. In other words, seeing as He is the Creator of all things, and predicts what eventually will be referred to as history; hundreds, even thousands of years ahead of time; how can Israel even think that He is overlooking them? Or that they are somehow hidden from Him? Or disregarded by God? If the Creator Who is Just and Righteous; if He punished His Own people because of their sin; He Who does not show favoritism but punishes the sins of all; how could He then, overlook, disregard, His Own people if they are repenting and sorry for their sin, now that the evil is being purged out of them?

Israel needed His Arms to work in their favor. They needed an embrace that would reassure them He was still their God. So God sent His prophet Isaiah, to not only shout of the discipline that was in store, but to also shout out the salvation that would not only see Israel restored to her former glory, but a future glory that would include all nations, prophesying of the Christ! They asked for a hug, and they received a HUG!! By a nation, led by King Cyrus who "Spanked" them, they would also receive Deliverance…a "HUG"!

Sad to say, but sometimes I get P.L.O.M. disease. That's an acronym for Poor Little Old Me. Sometimes I feel disregarded by God. Sometimes I would just like a hug. Or, maybe everything is just peachy. But I just feel kind of low. Well today I'm not going to wait for someone to notice! Before this day ends I am going to ask someone for a hug. I'm not just going to go hug someone. I'm going to ASK someone for a hug. I'll keep it pure. I'll be wise in who I ask. I'm going to allow God to "hug" me through another. Allow God to work through someone by giving me a hug. Allow a request by me to a brother/sister for a hug; have THEM be used by God, to encourage ME!

OCTOBER 22-28

Romans 3:22–24

Three verses to memorize which contain a plain and simple message.

How many have sinned and need Christ?

I guess that includes me...

On that note, I want to finish Isaiah today in my readings. I feel like my prayers have been getting kind of routine, so I'm going to use a couple of psalms this week to correct that. I'll read them, instead of having a regular Bible reading, to help me get in a prayerful mood. Then I'm going to start reading my second favorite book of the Old Testament which is Jeremiah. So I'll start my week by finishing up Isaiah by reading chapters 52-66, a couple of days I'll use a Psalm, so I'll choose Psalm 142 and 143, then I'll finish up the week by reading the first 4 chapters of Jeremiah. So that's...

Isaiah 52–66
Psalm 142-143
Jeremiah 1–4

I really enjoyed reading Isaiah. So much that I just read and didn't pray. But that's ok, because I'm not checking off a list of "to dos" when it comes to communicating with God. Besides, He was communicating so well to me through Isaiah that I just couldn't stop listening, and then I had to get a move on to begin my day. My thoughts, as I'm reading, are constantly going back and forth to Him anyways, so I am communicating with Him. I know I'll have the same problem with Jeremiah. But it's a great problem to have! That's why I've thrown a couple of psalms in this week.

Like I have written previously, Isaiah is my favorite Old Testament book. God uses such descriptive words, at times so very poetic, as He predicts Israel's downfall because of His Justice, and as He predicts her return to Him because of His great Mercy. I read how He is dismayed by Israel, disappointed that He has to raise His hand in discipline against her. Then how He tenderly longs for her return, and will do everything He can to bring her back to Him in such a way that she will never be lost to the other nations again. He accomplishes this by giving of Himself, in the embodiment of Christ, which is predicted in the writings of Isaiah hundreds of years before it takes place.

God is amazing, and every time I take the time to study, not just read, but study His Word, I find it is the most amazing literature I have EVER read. I believe it's because of the simple fact that He Who created us knows our inmost parts, and therefore knows, like no one else can ever know, how to meet our needs in every way, and can communicate to those needs, through His Word, filling them beyond even our own wildest expectations. But there is a clue in Isaiah 55:1-11 as to the attitude I must have when reading His Word; especially verses 8-9 of that passage. I must try to think in a new way. His Ways bear no resemblance to worldly ways.

From the day I was born, I have had worldly ideas and worldly ways crammed down my throat whether I wanted it or not. From every direction, educators, the media, all are cramming things into my heart. No wonder, as I get older, it is a constant walk of perseverance to keep my eyes focused on God. It's so important, that every time I open my Bible, I must clear my mind, grab hold of God's Word, and read it as if someone I do not know, is communicating something to me that I have longed to know all my life, but never have. I need to be like this so I will keep learning, no matter how old I get, or how many times I read my Bible. Then each time, because my heart is open, God is able to communicate to me His way, which often is a totally new way of thinking. It is based on love, joy, peace, patience, kindness, goodness, faithfulness, gentleness and self-control. When I have this attitude every time I read, His Word is to my soul like a constant thirst-quencher, filling me to satisfaction, accomplishing everything God desires to occur within me.

That's why I like this particular passage. He guarantees that will take place if I have the right attitude. Actually, He guarantees that His Word will accomplish His Will even if I don't have the right attitude. But then I believe His Word accomplishes a different task, that of hardening hearts that don't want to listen. That's another topic. Whatever, His Word will not come back empty, but it accomplishes His Will. Not my guarantee...His.

Two ideas just came to me, something I can do to impress this passage upon my heart in a practical way. I came up with one idea at first, but then felt I might not be brave enough, so I came up with a second idea.

Here's the second idea, the one I came up with in case I'm not feeling very brave. Sometime this week I'll take someone I don't know very well, out for lunch; pay for everything.

If I'm really feeling brave, my first idea was to go to a mall, and find a complete stranger, or a couple, and buy them lunch; pay for everything. I'll tell them it's just something I want to do because of kindness that has been shown to me. They won't understand. It'll be totally new to them. They might even be afraid. It may even be hard to find someone. People just don't do this out of the kindness of their heart...do they?

What it will do for me is help me to understand this passage. God offers His Word to everyone; some accept it; some are afraid; and some just can't be bothered. It must make Him sad.

So I'm going to offer something for free. I'm sure some will be afraid not trusting me to pay for everything; some just won't want to be bothered; but hopefully someone will accept. Either way, what I'm offering will accomplish what I intend; it will show me where their hearts are.

OCTOBER 29-NOVEMBER 4

Romans 6:3–4

I love these verses. I am going to love writing these on my heart. Here it is revealed as to how I actually obeyed the Gospel. The Gospel is the good news about the death, burial, and resurrection of Jesus Christ. I understand that I am to obey the Gospel. How? How can I obey the death, burial, and resurrection of Jesus Christ?

These verses reveal how water baptism re-enacts the death, burial, and resurrection of Jesus Christ. I die to my sins (repentance), I am then buried with Him in the water (baptism), and I rise up out of the water to walk in newness of life. A death, a burial, and a resurrection—is that not amazing?

Oh, by the way. After meditating on these verses, I came to realize something. According to this passage, when I was baptized, there were three in the water; me, the person doing the baptizing—and Jesus.

Wow! Now that is amazing! Ok, ok; now for this week's readings. I'll be continuing in Jeremiah, reading chapters 5-24, and maybe leave it at that. Wait. Maybe I'll read some psalms this week too. Read them before I pray. I'll use Psalm 144-147; the four of them. So again...

Jeremiah 5–24
Psalm 144-147

Jeremiah 6:15-17 are three verses written in the context of a very sad time in the history of Israel. The Lord, speaking to His people through His prophet Jeremiah, states that they had become so sinful they had even forgotten how to blush. Nothing was shameful to them.

I wonder if some of the things that are acceptable to me would have offended people about 50 years ago; time to visit some old and wise people. I'm going to visit someone elderly; someone who has grown up in a totally different era than me. As I spend time with them I'll ask about how people dressed when they were young. What was considered inappropriate in their day; ask them about different freedoms I have or take today compared to their days. Perhaps about dating, or what they did for entertainment. I'm curious to what their answers may be. Perhaps everything is pretty much the same, or, perhaps in some ways, I have forgotten how to blush.

NOVEMBER 5-11

Romans 10:9

This is a favorite verse for those who want to turn love away from God and onto them. They'll state that you don't need to be baptized in order for your sins to be forgiven. "Read it," they'll say. "Where does it mention baptism?" To which I'll say, "Back in Romans 6:3–4 is where it mentions baptism. Did you forget so soon?"

This passage is not discussing the point in time I become saved; it is discussing how I am to maintain a saving faith. Paul is not writing this letter to unbelievers. He's writing it to Christians in Rome; see the beginning of the letter. That's why in Rom. 6:3–4 he doesn't command them to be baptized, he reminds them of when they were baptized.

This letter is written to people who have followed the teachings of Christ as given to them by the apostles of whom Paul was one. Paul's revelation in this letter of the majority of the Jews being lost was alarming to the Gentiles. If the majority of Jews who were known as God's people ended up not being saved, then how can we (Gentiles) who were aliens to the covenant be saved? Before and after this verse Paul had to encourage his readers to maintain their walk in Christ and they would be saved. Had the Jews believed that Jesus was the Christ and confessed Him as such, they too would have been saved, as they would have devoted themselves to His teachings and been baptized the same way these Christians were back in Romans 6:3–4.

This verse, Rom. 10:9, is not to be taken as what I must do to begin salvation. That is not the context in which it is written. It is to be taken as what I must do to maintain salvation. Must I submit to the rules of the Law of Moses to be saved? No! Must I do a checklist of works to make sure I am saved? No! Now that I have been baptized, if I sin, do I fall from grace? Do I have to do something to be saved all over again? No! If I have been baptized into Christ, in order to maintain my salvation I need to continue to confess Jesus is Lord and believe God raised Him from the dead. Nothing more is needed, my salvation is assured. For if I continue to confess Him as My Lord, my walk will reflect such; and if I truly believe God has raised Him from the dead, I also will be raised from the dead.

That is so comforting because there are times when I don't feel God is close to me. When I struggle with sin; when friends or relatives die in unexplainable and sometimes very painful ways; when close friends betray me; when I suffer terrible sickness; if my faith is demonstrated by how I feel, I would give up. But this verse reveals to me that no matter how I may feel, even if I am confessing Jesus is Lord and believing He was indeed raised from the dead while they nail me to a cross for such a belief, I know, beyond any doubt, because God always holds true to His Word, I will be saved!

That's amazing!

I'm going to dedicate this week of Bible readings to the Psalms and Jeremiah. Let's see, I'll read Psalm 148-150, then some of Psalm 119. It's huge so I'll break it up. I'll read Psalm 119 verses 1 to 40. I'll also read Jeremiah chapters 25 to 44. Yeah! Good reading!

Psalm 119:1-40
Psalm 148-150
Jeremiah 25–44

I've had them; many times.

Say what?

Had what many times?

Oh, sorry. I was just meditating on a couple verses I will be reading this week.

Good days…when I just "feel" so good about my relationship to God. Days when I "know" He has blessed me immensely. Days that turn into nights when I look around from my bed my heart filled with joy, laying my head back with a sigh of peace and contentment. Nights where a song of rejoicing is in my heart and mind for all the good things that have come from God. My bedroom; where the lights go out, and I sigh with contentment; where I pray in secret to God and He rewards my prayers. Kind of like what is written in Psalm 149:4-5.

I'm going to buy something new for my bedroom this week; maybe a picture, or a new set of sheets, or a new pillow, or a stuffed animal or some other decorative item. Then from my bed I'll make it a point to rejoice in my heart, sing a quiet song to God, and thank Him for all His blessings.

NOVEMBER 12-18

Romans 12:1–2

I have spoken with many who came to Canada from foreign countries who have never properly mastered the English language. I have equally spoken with many of the same who have mastered the English language. I asked one how he had managed to master the language in so short a time when others take so long. He told me it was because when he went home, whenever anyone would speak to him in his native language, he would ask them in English to speak to him only in English. He refused to speak anything but English. He also told me he had many friends who were still struggling with the English language because when they went into their homes they spoke only in their native tongue. He did not renounce his language. In fact he has made sure his children are able to speak both his native language and English. He just decided to immerse himself in the English language because he knew if he did this his mind would gradually take on the English language and it would become natural to him. Then he would readily be able to understand the will of his fellow workers and he would be pleasing to them.

Well, well, well. Let's see if that can be applied to these verses.

The passage above that I am going to memorize this week is written about living out lives as a form of worship. I am not to conform to the pattern of the world, but to renew my mind.

So let's say I go into my home and immerse myself into a worldly lifestyle. Then I wonder why it is so hard to understand what God's will is for my life. Yet what if when I went into my home I practiced God's will? What if I regularly immersed myself into His Word? What if at the dinner table I talked about His will as a natural part of any discussion? Would it not have the same results as the young man I wrote about at the beginning? Would I not gradually take on His will; would not His will become natural to me?

That's why I'm memorizing verses. That's why I'm reading from His Word each week. That's why I'm meditating on certain passages and practically applying them in situations that will take me out of my comfort zone and put me into His zone where I will find real comfort. So I will be transformed and come to understand His will. I want to have a love for God that is a natural part of my life.

I'm going to stay in the psalms again this week, but just Psalm 119. I'll read verses 41-152. Along with that I'll finish up Jeremiah by reading chapters 45-52 and start Ezekiel. I really like the first half of the book of Ezekiel; the second half? not so much. Lot of measuring gets done. I'll read Ezekiel chapters 1-11 for this week.

Psalm 119:41–152
Jeremiah 45–52
Ezekiel 1–11

Some proclaim a different God of the Old Testament. They proclaim an angry God wrote the Old Testament and a loving God wrote the New Testament. But He is One and the Same. God's same judgment can be seen in the New Testament times with the destruction of Jerusalem, 70 A.D., and the eventual downfall of Rome…same God. The problem is people turn from God. People turn to evolution and believe we just suddenly or slowly over a billion years, evolved. People forget about God, until trouble comes, then expect Him to help, giving what we want when we want it. If I believe I came from a puddle of slime, the next time I'm in deathly trouble I should pray…

"Oh great puddle of slime, please hear my prayer and deliver me."

Understand, Ezekiel 9:1-11 is God's Right Judgment on Israel because of all her detestable practices. It's not JUST that they were worshipping idols, and turning from God's Law. It is also what they had become as a result of turning to idols and away from His Law. There was murder in the streets; the entire land was full of injustice. You see, when people turn away from the Words of the Creator, Who knows what is needed, the eventual result is total corruption. God pleaded with Israel way longer than any human would have. This is Him executing His judgment because He knows they are lost and will NOT turn back. Note: the ones who are friends of God will be spared; those who lament at all the injustice within their society. The others…? Not so good.

I believe I may have a friend who prays to a puddle of slime. It's time to pass on an invitation for a coffee.

It's time for a talk.

NOVEMBER 19-25

Romans 12:5

There it is again—one body, one church. Some may say that this verse is referring to many different groups, or churches. Nope. Keep it in its context. Paul is not writing here about many different groups. He's writing about each person. He is addressing this to every one of them. He writes about different gifts each person might have and encourages them to grow in those gifts. But the main point here is no one is an island. I should not think I can be a Christian all by myself. It is true that even if I am all by myself, I still need to maintain my Christianity, but when push comes to shove, when I have the choice of either being with the saints or being apart from them, I must choose to be a part. For according to this verse, I do not belong to myself, I belong to my brothers and sisters in Christ, and I am to use the gift(s) God has given me in service to Him/them. This is another good verse to commit to memory.

Psalm 133:1

I'm going to memorize this one too for the week. It doesn't need comment. Unity is good and pleasant. I need to strive for such.

To the point! So are my readings for this week; Ezekiel, chapters 12 to 28.

Ezekiel 12–28

As Isaiah is my favorite Old Testament writing, Ezekiel is my least favorite. Not because I disagree with God's Discipline of His children, but because I don't like reading about it. Ezekiel is God speaking with no holds barred. He lets it all out. And as He is the Master of Communication, His Words are blunt, to the point, and once again, right on the mark. God's Word in Ezekiel makes me cringe, as an example, Ezekiel 14:12-23. I need to read and meditate on passages such as these. I must not ignore them. Because what happened to Israel is what all deserve, because of sins. If not for Christ, I would be at the end of these words. I would like to be able to say...

"No, I would be like Noah, Daniel, and Job."

That's what I would like to be able to say, however, after personal study of these three men I find myself far removed from them when it comes to faith in God. All sin must meet punishment, and although the righteousness of Noah, Daniel, and Job may have saved themselves from a physical judgment on a city, their own righteousness would not save them from the wrath of God on sin in personal judgment on them, even if they only had once sinned. No, they too need Christ. However, the righteousness of individuals can save a city, even a nation from destruction. God will cease His judgment based on the righteousness of people in that city/country/nation. But Israel had become so bad, that even if these three were within her walls, only they, not even their loved ones, but only THEY would escape the wrath God was pouring out. And all this time some people think Noah and Job were just metaphorical men; that they never really existed.

Hmmmm.

Seems God figures they existed. But in all this terror, look at verses 22-23. There is good behind every action of God. He does this so that there will be a remnant that survives. Christ was promised through the seed line of Abraham. David was promised a Son that would forever sit on his throne. God still loved mankind, but if He allowed Israel to continue as she was that Promise made to Abraham would never come about. God doesn't break His Promises. However Israel had broken hers. God knew it would take some dreadful surgery to clean her up so that He could bring about the Promise "all nations shall be blessed through your seed" which He made to Abraham.

By the way, look at the end of verse 22. Even the animals suffer because of man's sin.

I'm going to visit an animal shelter and ponder these verses while I spend time there.

NOVEMBER 26 – DECEMBER 2

Deuteronomy 18:21–22

Many claim to be prophets today, and make predictions. But I need to memorize this verse because it reveals that every prophet in the Old Testament who was from God, whatever they prophesied, came true; even in the case of Jonah preaching destruction to the inhabitants of Nineveh. For his message was "repent, or you will be destroyed," and the people repented, thereby escaping destruction. It wasn't that God's message from His prophet didn't come about, for as sure as the prophet predicted, had they not repented, destruction of Nineveh would have followed.

So it would appear then that it is of prime importance that I know if a prophet is from God or speaking on his own.

Is his message from God if he is 60% right?

Is his message from God if he is 70% right?

How about 99%?

Try 100%.

Readings are simple for this week. I want to get through Ezekiel. I'll want to make sure I read Ezekiel chapters 29-48 when I'm not tired. God wants me to understand what took place here. I need to read these chapters carefully.

Ezekiel 29–48

Edom...those of Seir...the brother of Israel...Esau; they watched Israel, their brother, fall. They enjoyed it. It was to their benefit...so they thought. In Ezekiel 35:1-15 God says, "Nope." Of all the nations, they should not have rejoiced. Jacob's brother, Edom. So now it will be even worse for them, because they turned their back on their brother.

Look at verse 13. They were speaking against Israel, not God. However God makes it clear, "you speak against Israel, My children, you speak against Me."

I need to make sure I never treat a brother or sister in Christ this way. I need to make sure I never feel a little bit of joy in my heart when someone I don't get along very well with gets caught in sin. Or find a little joy in my heart when they don't do well in something they planned for the church.

I think I may have at one time or another.

Shame on me...those feelings were against God, and He saw it. Perhaps it's not too late. I'll phone them; admit it to them. How can I begin to tell them? I'm not sure, but a good start will be, "Hello?"

DECEMBER 3-9

Isaiah 55:1–2

Israel had their temptations. They longed to be like the other nations around them. To make themselves more acceptable to the other nations, they became like them, instead of being an example to the nations, so that they, the other nations, by Israel's example, would become godly. Instead, Israel indulged in the same kind of immorality as the other nations. Even worse, they accepted the other gods of other nations, even bowing down to them—idolatry. Yet all this, in their desire to be "liked" by other nations, instead of making them acceptable, actually made them detestable. Israel became even lower than a prostitute to the other nations, becoming dependant on them, giving herself freely to the other nations for their pleasure, so that she became an offense to God, as well as to the other nations. All the while, God was begging through His prophets for Israel to come back to Him, where all the desires of their hearts had been met before and could be met again.

These will be two good verses for me to memorize. Today has a temptation of its own. It may not be God's people wanting to be like other nations, but it sure could be God's people wanting to be popular/like other people—those in the world. To turn to what they turn to, their gods: looking for satisfaction from alcohol or drugs, which are many times, if not all the time, associated with immorality. The message is still the same.

Instead of prophets, today the Word of God is almost everywhere, begging me to turn to a better way of life—God's Way. Why spend money on alcohol and drugs that make me dependant so that I need to keep going back for more until there is no money left? Slavery comes at a high price—higher than one may think. Whether to the gods of another nation, or the addictions of the world, my soul is the cost. All the while I have the greatest offer from the greatest God, the One and only, and all I have to do is "listen to Him."

He has a love for me...do I have a love for God?

Daniel had a great love for God. I think I'll read the book of Daniel this week, chapters 1-12. I want a psalm to read before I pray, well, maybe just a few lines before I pray, Psalm 119:153-160. The memory verses I'm committing to memory have left me a little curious. I'm going to start into Hosea and read chapters 1-7. It'll shed some light on just how far from God Israel had drifted.

Daniel 1–12
Psalm 119:153–160
Hosea 1–7

Daniel 2:1-49 is an amazing history lesson given by the prophet Daniel, especially seeing as he gives this class to Nebuchadnezzar BEFORE the history takes place! What is even more amazing is the request the king makes. He doesn't tell Daniel the dream and then ask him to interpret it. He asks Daniel to tell him the dream, and then interpret it! And Daniel does! Amazing!

I read this today, and am able to see the historical accuracy in Daniel's interpretation. The four great empires! Babylonians, Medes/Persians, Greeks, and finally, the fourth, Rome! And in the time of that fourth kingdom, Rome, God would establish His kingdom; and He did! Christ was born, lived, and was crucified, then raised from the dead to be crowned King of kings, Lord of lords, over a kingdom that would never end!

Amazing pre-history lesson!

Know what?

I'm going to do something this week I haven't done for a long time; go to a museum; either by myself or with a group. Just to check out some history.

DECEMBER 10-16

Isaiah 59:1–2

I want these two verses written on my heart. God is always within arm's reach; He's only an ear-shot away. It is never Him Who moves, but I. Before I can expect Him to hear and help I have to do something about the element that is blocking communication with Him—my sins. I've been baptized, so my sins have been taken away. Now I need to continue to walk in the Light confessing and being sorry for my sins. I want Him to hear my prayers.

For readings this week I'll finish up Hosea and read chapters 8-14, then start right in on Amos and read chapters 1-9. Then back to the New Testament, Revelation chapters 1-4.

Hosea 8–14
Amos 1–9
Revelation 1–4

Revelation 3:20 is sometimes used as an authority for the false teaching that people who are unbelievers can have Christ come into their hearts just by "asking Him to come in". I guess there's something to be said for a person when they want someone to be saved they'll misquote Scripture...NOT!

Look.

God's not playing a game where I can make up my own rules as I go along. I need to remember that satan wants everyone in hell with him, just to hurt God, and will go to any means to do it. He will trick, deceive, and cheat...anything and everything...no holds barred! And if I do not follow the directions as given by the Holy Spirit through Jesus Christ and His apostles...I...will...lose.

Because at the end of time, at the judgment scene, satan will be right there accusing me of not following God's Word. Perhaps he'll yell out,

"If you let that person into heaven when they didn't follow your teachings, and they taught others not to follow your teachings, then what right do you have to condemn me? If I'm condemned, then they should be too!"

Read Revelation 3:20.

I mean it!

Right now!

Read it!

Who is it written to?

Look at the context.

Read the beginning of 3:14.

This is written to the church.

This is written to people in the church.

This is written to Christians.

This is how a Christian who has fallen away, who has become apathetic to the cause of Christ, who has walked away from Christ, comes back into a right relationship with Christ.

This is NOT teaching how someone who is not a Christian becomes a Christian.

It IS teaching how a Christian who has fallen away, whose love has become "phony" to Christ, makes things right again. He/she doesn't have to be baptized again, all they need do is open the door of their hearts and allow Christ BACK into their lives.

I know some people who have been tricked by the false teaching of "praying Jesus into their heart".

It's time for a phone call.

DECEMBER 17-23

Isaiah 64:6–7

These verses, written on my heart, will remind me that all the righteous deeds, if I have sin in my life, are as filthy rags to God. I must first get rid of the sins, so that He may see the righteous deeds. "In Him" I am seen as righteous, pure, without sin. But I must be "in Him."

Another verse I have already memorized taught me that when I am baptized into Him I am clothed with Him. ..I am in Him.

I remembered it!

I memorized it!

My love for God is becoming a natural part of my life!

That's exciting!

Reassuring!

On to the weekly readings!

This week plenty of variety! I'll read Revelation chapters 5-10; continue with the prophets and read Micah 1-7, Haggai 1-2, and Zechariah 1-4. I'll use Psalm 119:161-168 and Psalm 81 to help me get in a prayerful mood. It's coming up to that time of year, so I'll read Matthew chapters 1-3! I absolutely love this time of year!

Revelation 5-10
Micah 1–7
Psalm 81
Psalm 119:161–168
Haggai 1–2
Zechariah 1–4
Matthew 1–3

It is all starting to come together!

As I read; as I pray; as I write His Word on my heart!

I read Matthew 1:18-25. I am reminded of another passage that we who once were aliens and foreigners to the covenant, now because we are in Christ, by His Promise, have become His people, saved from our sins. We who once were neighbors, now because we are in Christ, by His Promise, have become His people, saved from our sins...who were once neighbors...neighbors!

I have a love for God!

I have learned to love Him the way He longs to be loved!

I WANT to invite my neighbors over for supper this week!

DECEMBER 24-31

Ezekiel 18:20

This final verse for the year that I am going to commit to memory, quite simply reveals, sins are not charged against me that I personally do not commit. Now, that is not to say the consequence of my sin does not hurt others. But I must be careful not to mix up the two. God will hold each individual accountable, but only for their personal sins. However, the consequences of those sins may be visited down even to the third and fourth generation, who may think God is punishing them for prior generations. But it is not necessarily God punishing the third or fourth generation, but is a natural result of the sins of the first generation.

For instance, let's say I get mixed up in a wild lifestyle, or get involved with a lifestyle of crime, or perhaps am just lazy. I get married and raise a family that follows the example I have set. This can carry on for several generations...and it all began with me!! Perhaps someone will break away from this pattern, but even if they do not follow the sinful lifestyle, they may, as a consequence of my sinful decisions, suffer. But that is not to say they themselves are being disciplined by God for my sins. They are naturally reaping the consequences of my sins. There is a big difference between the consequence of personal sin to my own life and the consequence of my sins and how they may affect others who are innocent. It is only personal sin for which I will have to give an account to God. Of course, if I get "into Christ," even the condemnation as a result of my personal sins can be taken away.

Readings for the final week! When I finish these I will have read my entire Bible! Now if you started in the middle of the year you won't be as excited as I am, but hey...this is exciting! Plus I have all these verses written on my heart! Ok, settle down. What's left? I'll finish the psalms by reading Psalm 49 and 63. I've already read the last chapters of Mark and Luke but I saved the first chapters for this time of year. I did the same for Matthew and read the first three chapters last week! So this week I'll read Mark 1-4 and Luke 1-4. I'll finish the prophets by reading Zechariah 5-14 and Malachi 1-4. I'll finish Revelation by reading chapters 11-20...no...I didn't forget chapters 21-22. I already read them at the beginning of the year as it has to do with new beginnings so it goes better with the first week of the New Year! I did it! I did it! HE DID IT!

Psalm 49
Psalm 63
Mark 1–4
Luke 1–4
Revelation 11-20
Zechariah 5–14
Malachi 1–4

God often uses the bride/groom/covenant relationship between Himself and His people. I am never to tire of my relationship to Him. I am never to break covenant with Him because I tire of Him. I am never to forget the love I had for Him when I first came to Him. His love for me will never change. My love for Him may, but His for me will never. According to Malachi 2:13-16, it is the same for wives/husbands. A covenant is entered upon in marriage. It isn't "until you are no longer beautiful." It isn't "until you are no longer healthy." It isn't "until I no longer have feelings for you." IT WAS "until death do us part."

Get out some picture albums/digital photographs.

Sit down with your spouse.

Look at them together.

Remember.

The body wears out, but inside the needs are still the same.

She/he is your marriage partner, the wife/husband of your marriage covenant.

The New Year is close upon us...let's begin it right...